Edited by John Laker.

Authorship - The many, many members of Archaeology In Marlow, local people and professional and amateur academics who helped to compile this book.

Colour photographs taken by John Laker, Julie Rushton, or Arthur Boarder.

ROMADAM Project Co-ordinators - David Greenwood and John Laker.

This publication was funded by the Local Heritage Initiative.

The Local Heritage Initiative is a national grant scheme that helps groups to investigate, explain and care for their local landscape, landmarks, traditions and culture. The Heritage Lottery Fund (HLF) provides the grant but the scheme is a partnership, administered by the Countryside Agency with additional funding from Nationwide Building Society.

For more information see HLF's website - www.hlf.org.uk

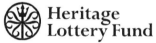

Printed in the UK by Wycombe District Council, Queen Victoria Road, High Wycombe, HP11 1BB.

Published by Archaeology In Marlow, c/o 9 Spinfield Lane, Marlow, SL7 2JT.

To contact Archaeology In Marlow, write to the above address, or visit our website - www.archaeologyinmarlow.org.uk

First published 2008.

ISBN 978-0-9559682-0-4

# Introduction

Archaeology is the ultimate detective story because there are generally just a few clues which often do not add up! Consequently, when the few pieces of the jig-saw are put together, a selection of different theories tends to be put forward by the archaeological detectives.

In 2003 a group of archaeological detectives got together to investigate our history and pre-history (before written records) in and around Marlow. The group called itself *Archaeology In Marlow* (AIM).

To help achieve its objectives, AIM formed a plan to investigate four earthworks close to Marlow. The plan was developed over 18 months and became the ROMADAM Project. ROMADAM is an acronym for the *Recording Of Marlow And District's Ancient Monuments*. AIM submitted the plan to the Local Heritage Initiative (LHI), applying for a grant to fund the Project. Subsequently, AIM was very fortunate to receive a generous award of £22,605 to conduct the ROMADAM Project.

AIM researched all four monuments in the Project, recorded their physical features and surveyed their topography. The ROMADAM Project ran for just over three years and involved many AIM members and others who had interests in the sites.

# The ROMADAM Project

Within a mile or two of Marlow are four important earthworks of varying ages. Whether or not you are interested in historical sites, they are all in both beautiful and tranquil parts of our local countryside and are just waiting for you to visit and enjoy. Most Marlow people will have heard of 'the trenches', but few will have seen the other three archaeologically interesting sites.

Prior to being awarded a grant from Local Heritage Initiative, now the Heritage Lottery Fund (HLF), AIM made a proposal to research and record the following four sites:

- The Iron Age Hill Fort, Medmenham, west of Marlow (National Grid Reference [NGR] SU8069:8467)

- The First World War Training Trenches at Pullingshill Wood, Marlow Common (NGR SU8216:8630)

- A Circular Earthwork of uncertain age at Warren Wood, Little Marlow (NGR SU8715:8972)

- The Iron Age Hill Fort at Danesfield, west of Marlow (NGR SU8176:8440).

AIM's investigations into these four sites were commenced in the same order as they appear above and the chapters in this book are also in the same order.

See Map 1, page ii, for locations.

# Map showing locations of all four ROMADAM sites

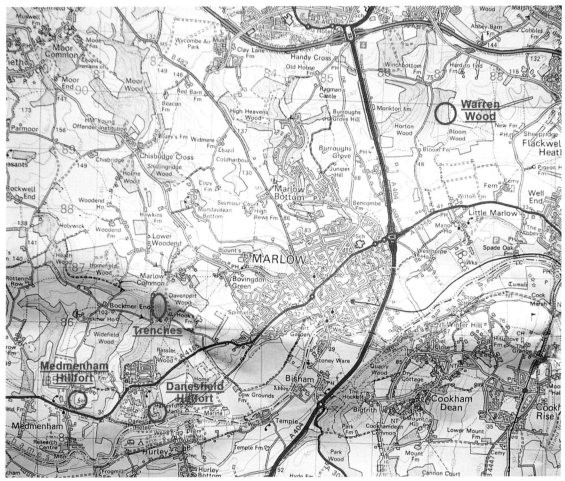

**Map 1** *(reproduced by permission of Ordnance Survey on Behalf of HMSO.© Crown copyright 2005. All rights reserved. Ordnance Survey License number 100044133)*

# Contents

### Archaeology In Marlow's ROMADAM Project

..............................

# Chapter One

## *The Iron Age Hill Fort at Medmenham*

The first ROMADAM Project monument to be investigated was the Iron Age Hill Fort at Medmenham, to the north-east of the Medmenham crossroads. National Grid Reference (NGR) SU8069:8467.

### Proposal

The Archaeology In Marlow proposal, put to Local Heritage Initiative, now the Heritage Lottery Fund, consisted of a plan to gather research into the Hill Fort and its castle, to survey the site and then produce a detailed plan showing the results.

AIM was also entrusted to produce this book describing the research and outcomes of the work, to use this information to produce a leaflet and to display an information panel to be placed in the Hill Fort, for the benefit of the Medmenham people and visitors to the area.

In addition, the results of the investigations would be passed to the four owners of the site, English Heritage and the Archaeology Department at Bucks County Council.

### The Location

Just off the crossroads at Medmenham (junction of Bockmer Lane, Ferry Lane and the A4155), diagonally opposite St Peter's Church, are the remains of a substantial Iron Age Hill Fort (see maps 2 and 3, pages 2 and 3, and photograph 1, page 2). There is a footpath on the east side of Bockmer Lane, which gives access to the Hill Fort, but it is somewhat steep and can be slippery! The footpath allows access to the western wooded side of the Hill Fort, but the eastern side, although clearly visible, is on private land and only accessible with the agreement of the landowners.

The Hill Fort is a Scheduled Ancient Monument and under the protection of English Heritage (Sites and Monuments Record No. 27140), so it is not permitted to dig up anything, or to take metal detectors onto the site.

### Purpose & Usage

The term 'Hill Fort' can be a little misleading as they are found in valleys, on plains, on promontories and on hills. Their shapes tend to depend on the lie of the local land, but they all have at least one bank and one ditch. The remaining earthworks at Medmenham have at least two banks and one ditch. Hill Forts exist all over the British Isles and appear to have had several different functions. They were first built in the late Bronze Age (about 1,000BC) and continued to be constructed up until the Roman invasion in 43AD. They all seem to have a defensive role. Some were used to store grain in numerous underground pits, whilst others were probably used to keep cattle and/or sheep safe from rival tribes. In some cases there is evidence of structures indicating protected settlements. Other Hill Forts were possibly used as high status

## Location of Medmenham Iron Age Hill Fort

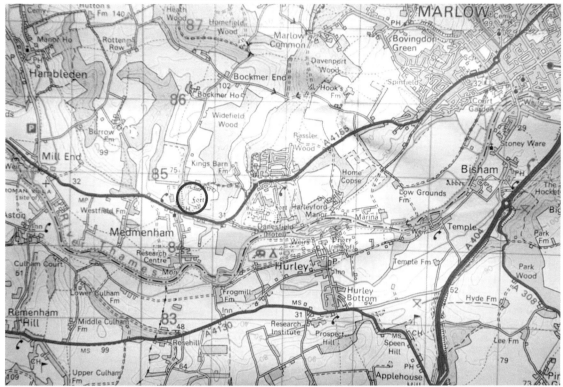

**Map 2** *(reproduced by permission of Ordnance Survey on Behalf of HMSO. © Crown copyright 2005. All rights reserved. Ordnance Survey License number 100044133)*

## Summit of north-western bank of Medmenham Hill Fort

**Photograph 1**

# 1973 Ordnance Survey map showing the outline of Medmenham Iron Age Hill Fort and the footpaths running across it and along its western bank - scale 1:2500

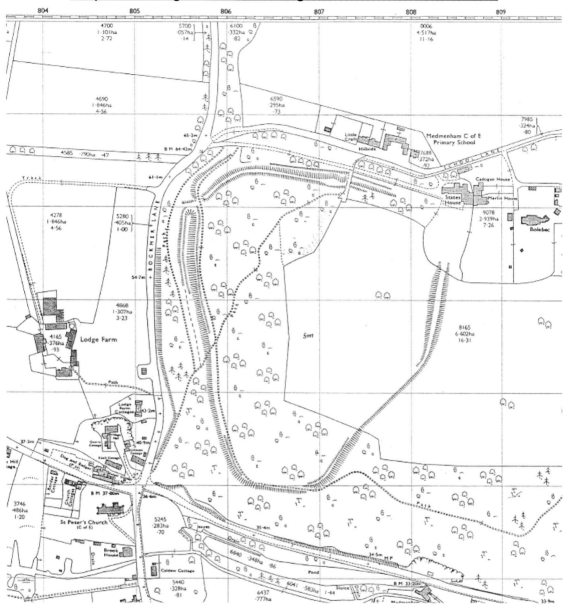

**Map 3**      *(reproduced by permission of Ordnance Survey on Behalf of HMSO. © Crown copyright 2005. All rights reserved. Ordnance Survey License number 100044133)*

residences of tribal chiefs and their families.

It is thought that Hill Forts were constructed over many years using basic tools such as, 'antler picks'. 'L-shaped' pieces of antler have been found at other Hill Fort sites and they would have been used to excavate ditches, with the excavated material being used to create the banks. Often palisades (defensive wooden walkways) were then built upon the inner bank for additional security.

The Medmenham Hill Fort lies north of the Thames, within the area occupied by the Catuvellauni tribe, or people. Opposite Medmenham, was the Atrebates tribe occupying the south side of the Thames. Neither of these tribes left any written evidence and little is known about them, prior to the writings of Roman historians.

Following the Norman invasion in 1066, the Manor of Medmenham became the property of Hugh de Bolebec. According to historians, Hugh, or perhaps one of his sons (Walter or Hugh II), built a castle within the Hill Fort that was subsequently known as Bolebec Castle.

At the top of the footpath, leading up from Bockmer Lane, near to Medmenham crossroads, visitors should see a board giving information on the Hill Fort.

**Topography, Geology and Flora**

The steep footpath leading up from the Medmenham crossroads bring visitors on to a plateau, an area of about 6.5 hectares of land that overlooks the Thames Valley. The Hill Fort varies in height from 100 to 125 metres above sea level and is 25 metres higher than the edge of the river Thames's flood plain below (see Maps 3 and 4 on pages 3 and 5). The underlying geology is of 'older river gravel', deposited by a previous ice age, lying over the natural 'upper chalk' bedrock.

There is a diverse selection of trees in the wooded area, with laurel, hazel, elder, yew, holly, sycamore, sweet chestnut, silver birch, oak, beech, cherry, field maple and ash. Where there is undergrowth, it consists of ferns, brambles, privet, hawthorn and dog rose.

Visitors will observe that approximately half of the Hill Fort is fairly densely wooded and the other half is now pasture. The eastern bank is now barely visible as it has been 'ploughed out' over the centuries, but a keen eye will spot the ridge that still remains. The most complete evidence of the Hill Fort's earthworks exists in the north-western corner of the site, overlooking Bockmer Lane.

Within the woods is evidence of quarrying; large pits can be seen, from which, clay, gravel, or chalk, have been removed

**Research**

AIM spent much time researching all four sites and listed below are the most important references relating to the Medmenham Hill Fort and the castle of the Bolebecs, which

**Medmenham Iron Age Hill Fort - Map taken from the Reverend Arthur Plaisted's 1925 book entitled, 'The Manor & Parish Records of Medmenham' showing the site of Bolebec's Castle**

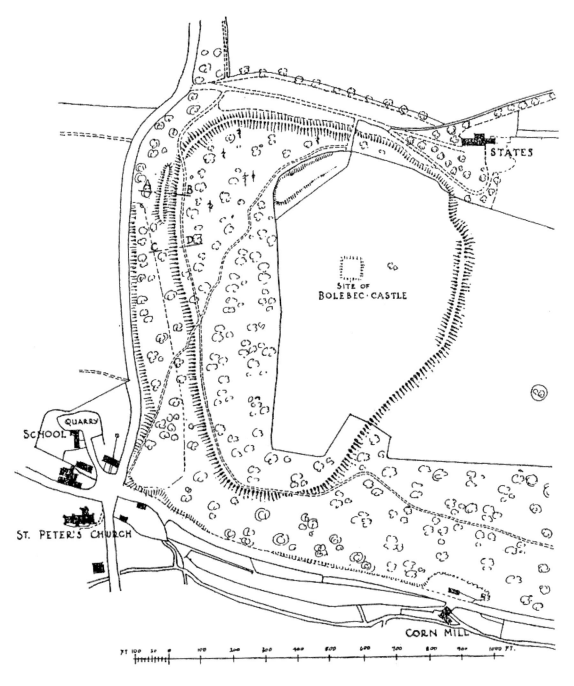

CAMP IN GILLMAN'S WOOD

SITE OF BOLEBEC·CASTLE

STATES

SCHOOL

QUARRY

ST. PETER'S CHURCH

CORN MILL

**Map 4**

was allegedly built within the Hill Fort. Observant visitors will notice that there is barely a kilometre between Medmenham Hill Fort, also known as Gillman's Camp, or Wood, and Danesfield Hill Fort (nearer to Marlow).

- In 1901, in *The Memorials of Old Buckinghamshire*, it says, 'here (at Medmenham) on a height commanding magnificent views of the river and surrounding country, De Bolebec built a castle, which, judging from the remaining earthworks and their large circumference, must have been a mighty stronghold.

- In 1912, in the *Royal Commission of Historic Monuments Vol. 1*, Bucks, an entry reads, 'Contour camp NE of church and SW of States House, is situated from 500 to 550 feet above O.D., and encloses an area of 16 acres. The defences consist of a single rampart and ditch except 100 yds on the W side where there is an outer bank. There are several old chalk and gravel pits. Original entrance appears to have been on the NW. Path on SW leads to spring. W rampart 15.5ft high 46.5ft wide, ditch 3.5ft deep, 44.5ft wide'.

- In 1925 in the *Victoria County History, Bucks, Vol III*, stated, 'Medmenham: Immediately to the north-east is a prehistoric contour camp, enclosing 16 acres which is fortified by a rampart and a ditch and on the west by an advanced rampart; there are several old gravel and chalk-pits on the site. On a hill to the north-east of Medmenham church is the supposed site of the castle or manor-house of the Bolebecs. There is a path down the hill to the spring below and the locality is known as 'States' or 'the States Farm'.

- *The Manor & Parish Records of Medmenham*, Plaisted 1925, 'This camp is of contour type, and it belongs to an age when people were becoming independent of natural fastnesses and were beginning to understand the value of protective works'. 'One original entrance appears to have been in the north-west, branching off the road now leading to States. On the south-west a path, protected by a bank, still leads from the entrenchments towards an ancient spring, which supplied the camp with water'. 'The stream from the village spring to New Lock continued to be identified until the nineteenth century as Bulbank's Ditch'. 'There can be no doubt that the Lordship House of Medmenham stood on the brow of the hill overlooking the Saxon settlement, within the entrenchments formed there by a prehistoric people'. 'These evidences have the witness of tradition, as well as the support of probability, and tradition also asserts that Hugh de Bolebec, or his immediate successors, rebuilt the Lordship House of Wlstan the thane, so that it became known thenceforth as Bolebec Castle'. 'Three centuries of cold neglect hastened the fate of the old manor house, which had been some time the residence of baron and earl; but it was still inhabitable in the sixteenth century'. 'The castle stood, according to tradition, in the field south of States, within the eastern rampart of the prehistoric earthworks and in this area the pavements referred to were no doubt unearthed'.

- In 1928 in the *Buckinghamshire Antiquities*, by Roscoe, he states,

'Medmenham. On a steep spur of high ground above the church, once the site of a castle, a farmhouse is boldly placed'.

- In 1932-3, *Memorials of Marlow, II - III*, by Colmer, he states, 'To the west (of Marlow), crowning the wooded eminence that overlooks the Thames at Medmenham, towered the stronghold of Hugh de Bolebec'.

- In 1951 and 1959, Letters in *Sites and Monuments Records* (SMR) file: Mr F M Underhill to Mr J F Head 31/3/51: 'The camp in Gillman's Wood is a pear-shaped earthwork with a single rampart and ditch except on the western side where the rampart is doubled in places. In the centre of the earthwork was the site of Bolebec's castle of which little is known. In Hearne's time (1700) some fragments of building still existed. When I last walked over the site (23/1/45) the interior of the camp was uncultivated and the site was riddled with rabbits and a few stray pieces of brick were showing.' Mr F M Underhill to Mr J F Head 11/9/59: 'The site is of course the earthwork in Gillman's wood which contains a square marked on the map as the site of Bolebec's Castle. I have walked over it several times, picking up scraps of medieval pottery and tile.'

- In 1958, in Plaisted's, *The Romance of a Chiltern Village*, he gives a very detailed account of the castle on pages 26 and 27; pages 28 and 29 mention a Bolebec castle at Whitchurch (Aylesbury). He also says that a trade route started at Windsor, then crossed the Thames at Harleyford, skirted Danesfield and Gillman's Wood (Medmenham), through Fawley and Henley and then on to Dorchester. A map of the camp in Gillman's Wood, includes the Castle Keep in the south-eastern corner and its legend states, 'Water was obtained by an ancient pathway down a sloping bank leading to a spring. The Normans solved that problem by building the Castle Keep on a mound where the water could be reached by sinking a well'. 'Along the boundary where Lodge Hill meets the field Little Warren an ancient barrow in the form of a long bank extends westwards from Bockmer Lane for 300ft'. 'On the hill north-east of the church is the traditional site of Bolebec Castle. The Bayeaux tapestry, depicting buildings, costumes, and ships about the time of the Norman conquest, shows that castles in those days were of timber not stone. Any outline of the Keep can no longer be traced, but it stood on a mound above the present Marlow road, near the 39th milestone,.....'. 'A small clearing in Gillman's Wood surrounded by a stockade encloses a garden for the hermitage, at one time the dwelling of a hermit or guilleman, which subsequently was rebuilt as a keeper's cottage'.

- In 1993 in Pevsner's *Buildings of Bucks*, he says, 'States House Iron Age hill-fort is also just north of the main road. A pear-shaped univallate fort, sited on a bluff over-looking the Thames'.

- In the 1995 SMR schedule *Medmenham No 27140*; this document gives a detailed description of the site. It also states, 'A bronze knife blade found on the south west rampart in 1959, is thought to be Bronze Age date. Building remains, perhaps those of a farmhouse, were recorded within the fort in the early 18th century; but although stray pieces of brickwork have occasionally come to light, the precise location of these structures remains unknown. It has been suggested that this is the site of the castle built by the Bolebec family in the mid 12th century, during the period of the civil war known as the Anarchy'.

- *St Peter and St Paul Church*, Medmenham leaflet: 'The chantry priest seems to have been a Guilleman (hermit) and his dwelling stood within the precincts of Bolebec Castle'. Hence, 'Gillman's wood'.

The close proximity of Medmenham and Danesfield Iron Age Hill Forts of similar ages is not really understood. It could have something to do with the Thames being a significant territorial boundary between two major tribes in the area, the Catuvellauni north of the Thames and the Atrebates south of the river. It is also reported that a major trade route went from the Windsor area, via Harleyford, Yewden and Henley, to Dorchester, where there is a significant Hill Fort and the one at Danesfield is a smaller version of this. The Hill Forts at Medmenham and Danesfield may, therefore, have occupied important positions on this route simultaneously, one immediately after the other, or even hundreds of years apart.

## Method and Implementation - The search for Bolebec's Castle (2005, 2006 & 2008)

The Project's aims were to enable the participants to use the geophysical equipment and understand the methods being used to try to discover the whereabouts of Bolebec Castle, mentioned in books on Medmenham, by the Rev. Arthur Plaisted, and others (see 'Research', above).

It is an essential part of any LHI project to involve as many local people as possible and to offer training at every level. So, with the aid of the LHI grant, AIM arranged a series of 'magnetometry and resistivity training days' at the Hill Fort to endeavour to locate 'Bolebec's Castle' (Norman era) which, allegedly, stood in the centre of the Hill Fort; as referred to in books written by local authors, and present on older maps, showing its alleged position (see Map 4, page 5, for graphic from Rev Arthur Plaisted's book of 1925, 'The Manor & Parish Records of Medmenham').

AIM also arranged another series of 'surveying training days' to conduct topographic (ground) surveys in order to produce accurate plans of the features that are still present on this site.

So, on three Sundays in March 2005, in January and February 2006 and in April 2008, 'training days' were arranged to show how magnetometry and resistivity could be employed in order to locate the suspected castle.

Magnetometry equipment measures the minute differences of the Earth's magnetic field. High magnetic readings tend to indicate burnt areas and ditches and low magnetic readings tend to indicate less magnetically enhanced areas.

Resistivity equipment measures the electrical resistance within the earth. High resistance readings indicate solid materials (walls, etc.) and low resistance readings indicate wet areas (ditches, etc.).

For the technically minded the equipment used is defined on the next page.

8

**Magnetometry:-** Bartington Grad 601/2 magnetometer in gradiometer configuration, Line spacing - 1m, Reading spacing 0.25 m, Grid size - 30 x 30m, Number of grids - 5, Processing - ArcheoSurveyor software.

Relationship of grids.
North at top.

```
                 5
                 4
        1   2    3
```

Grid references - South west corner SU80670:84681

**Resistivity:-** CIA/TR Systems Resistivity meter, Electrode configuration - Twin electrode, Probe spacing - 0.5m, Reading spacing - 0.5m, Grid size - 20 x 20m, Number of grids - 1, Processing - TR Systems and ArcheoSurveyor software, Relationship of grids - grid no. 1 in north east corner of magnetometry grid no. 2.

Grid references - North west corner SU 80706:84718; North east corner SU80725:84720.

Again for the technically minded, Resistivity was used at a density of 1 reading every 0.5 metres on an area of 20 x 20 metres. This was because the documentary source identified the location of the castle and the density of readings should detect walls of 0.5 metres in width and more.

Magnetometry was also used as it could identify the location of the castle by locating ditches over a wider area.

A magnetometry survey will not be able to detect small features and those, such as graves, which have fills, as they are magnetically undetectable. Similarly, earth resistance differences in the dampness of the soil are important and weather and soil conditions can change, making features which are detectable one day, undetectable shortly later. In general, if geophysical investigations have not found anything, it does not mean that there is nothing there.

To see resistivity and magnetometry surveying in action, see photographs 2 and 3 on page 10.

## 2005

A total of 17 AIM members, local people and one of the landowners helped our Trainers, Mr Roger and Mrs Sally Ainslie of Abingdon Archaeological Geophysics. Other interested parties also viewed proceedings during the three Training Days in 2005.

A week prior to the Training Days, 30 metre square grids had been set out on the site either side of the access track running north/south through the paddock area under investigation (see Map 5, page 11). The southern square next to the access track was so positioned as to include the position of the castle, as indicated on older maps (see Map 4, Page 5).

# Medmenham Iron Age Fort - Mr Roger and Mrs Sally Ainslie at ROMADAM Training Days in 2005 and 2006 demonstrating Resistivity (top photograph) and Magnetometry (bottom photograph) Surveying techniques

**Photographs 2 and 3**

# Medmenham Iron Age Hill Fort - Layout of squares selected for conducting resistivity and magnetometry investigations

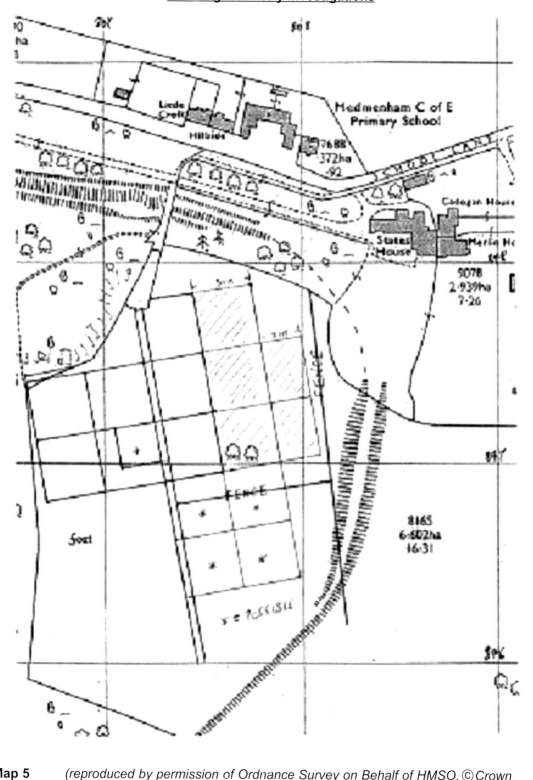

**Map 5** *(reproduced by permission of Ordnance Survey on Behalf of HMSO. © Crown copyright 2005. All rights reserved. Ordnance Survey License number 100044133)*

A total of seven 30 metre squares were laid out for geophysical surveys. Within the original western 30 metre square, one 20 metre square was subjected to a resistivity survey. Five of the 30 metre squares were subsequently surveyed using magnetometry.

The results gained from the magnetometry and resistivity surveys conducted in March 2005 did not locate the expected ditches but did identify pit-like features which could also be related to the locations of former trees. Magnetometry did not locate the ditch-like feature identified by resistivity (see figure 1, page 13).

## 2006

In January 2006, three 30 metre squares were marked out, as in 2005, plus two oblongs in the first field to the east of the gate and track. The vegetation, although mostly dead, was still relatively high and would have made both magnetometry and resistivity surveying difficult.

At the end of February one of the AIM members very kindly cut down the vegetation, enabling both magnetometry and resistivity surveys to be conducted on these three squares and two oblongs which had been marked out in the north-eastern field to the east of the gate and track, as in 2005.

Mr Ainslie was again the surveyor and he recommended that surveying should start in the south-eastern field, as this was covered in relatively short grass and would present fewer problems for magnetometry and resistivity surveying.

It was agreed to conduct a magnetometry survey and to extend the 30 metre squares, already marked out in the north-eastern field, into the south-eastern field. In a relatively short time Mr Ainslie was able to start the magnetometry work and after two hours, or so, he was able to display the results on his laptop computer (see figure 1, page 13).

The resistivity survey results were clearer, although the soil was so dry that the readings were all in the high range, as it shows a low resistance ditch-like feature cutting the higher resistance deposits and a pit-like anomaly. Unfortunately the area covered was not large enough to give a clearer picture of the nature of the anomalies which were identified.

In January and February 2006, surveying showed the Hill Fort's bank and traces of a ditch, but no trace of a building.

So, Mr Ainslie suggested that resistivity surveying should be tried on one square and a small strip of another square. This work took most of a bitterly cold day to conduct, but again in a short period of time Mr Ainslie was able to display the results on his laptop computer (see figure 1, page 13). These results were surprising! Again neither walls, nor ditches, were located, but evidence of a very wet area to the south of the trees! The opposite effect would normally be the case, so was there a 'dew pond', or pooling of water, which would otherwise drain freely into the plateau gravel? As rainwater quickly soaks away through porous chalk subsoils, dew ponds were often dug, generally lined

**Medmenham Iron Age Hill Fort - Resistivity Results and Magnetometry Results
recorded in 2005 and 2006 (North at top) superimposed on the 1973 Ordnance Survey map**

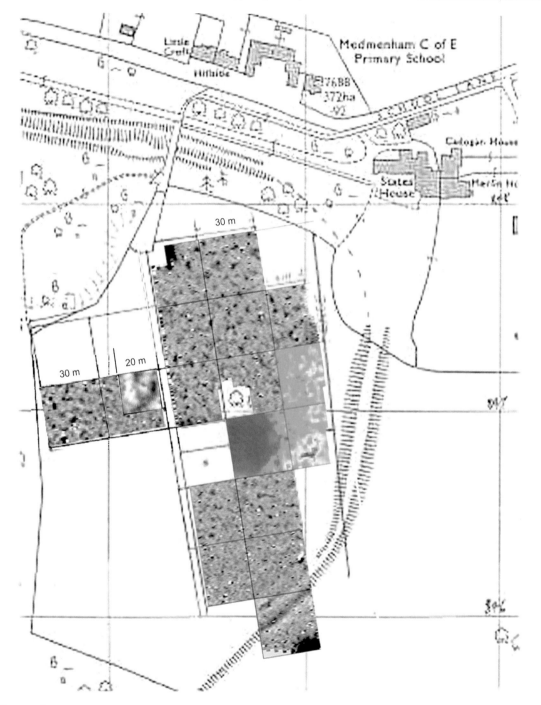

**Figure 1**    *(reproduced by permission of Ordnance Survey on Behalf of HMSO. © Crown
copyright 2005. All rights reserved. Ordnance Survey License number 100044133)*

Compilation graphic (figure 1), shows all the 30 metres squares, which were
surveyed with a magnetometer, except coloured squares and a smaller 20
metre square, which were surveyed using the resistivity equipment.

with clay, to provide a permanent water supply for thirsty livestock.

The magnetometry located pit-like features which could also be tree throw holes (pits caused when trees topple over and uproot). It also found possible linear features but these were largely obscured by the probable tree throw holes.

The resistivity result was different from the magnetometry, which shows that differences in magnetic characteristics of soil are not always the same as the differences in moisture content.

Mr Ainslie commented that the area had many pits, or tree throw holes. He initially thought that there was a 10m feature in the north-eastern field, but that had diminished with more processing. The extra processing had brought out a possible 45m diameter enclosure, like a banjo enclosure (see figures 2 and 3, page 15), but no trace of any ditches leading up to it were found. Also sundry other alignments and the Hill Fort ditches were clearly visible.

In conclusion, the anomalies which were located could have more to do with the Iron Age than the medieval period. There is not yet enough evidence to say that the feature is definitely 'a dew pond', but future investigations may prove its existence. However, the Castle was still elusive.

## 2008

In late April 2008, eight AIM members visited Medmenham Iron Age Hill Fort to conduct another 'Training Day'. This was devoted to trying to confirm the dowsers' previous positive predictions (see pages 24 and 28) as to the whereabouts of the elusive Bolebec's Castle (see map 4, page 5). AIM was very fortunate to attract another expert in resistivity and magnetometry surveying, Mr Geoff Deakin. Again 30 metre square grids were laid out the in the north-east field, followed by 20 metre squares, ready to accommodate Mr Deakin's magnetometry equipment (a 'Fluxgate Magnetometer – FM18 Geoscan). The 'trainees' then laid out ten 20 metre ropes across the first square, then the second, etc. These ropes were marked every metre to aid the process. Mr Deakin covered three squares, but on the forth square his equipment became adversely affected by the damp present on this wet and stormy morning.

On a beautifully warm sunny day in May 2008, six AIM members were joined by Mr Deakin for the very last ROMADAM Project 'Training Day' (see photograph 4, page 16). The intention was to conduct a magnetometry survey on the squares not completed in April. Again the 'trainees' laid out the grid of squares, as before, and then laid out the ropes in the fourth square ready for Mr Deakin to start. Mr Deakin completed another four squares. The results from these four squares and the results from the three squares previously surveyed, were combinod into one graphic (see figures 4 and 5, page 16).

## Method and Implementation - Surveying

The main aim was still to conduct a topographical survey (mapping the surface and

## Medmenham Iron Age Fort - 2006 Magnetometry uninterpreted (left graphic) and interpreted results (right graphic) showing likely features (North at top)

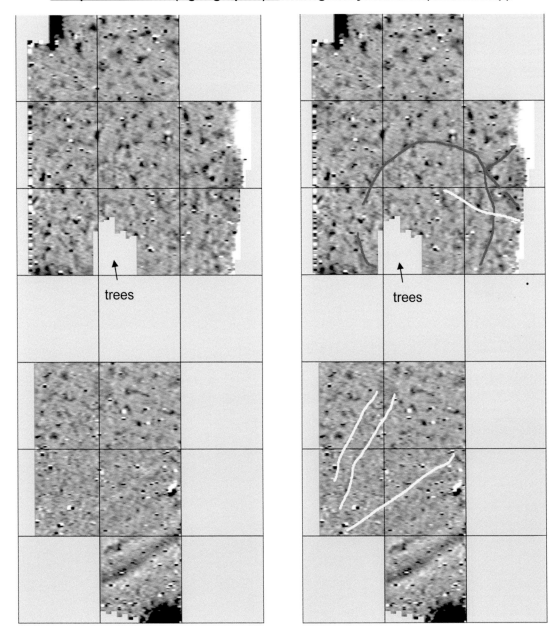

**Figure 2**                    **Figure 3**

The yellow lines on figure 3 are possible trackways and the red circular line may indicate an Iron Age Banjo Enclosure (so named from its shape).

# Medmenham Iron Age Hill Fort - Mr Geoff Deakin and volunteers at the very last ROMADAM Training Day in May 2008

**Photograph 4**

# Medmenham Iron Age Hill Fort - The very last Training Day in May 2008, showing the Magnetometry Surveying results produced by Mr Geoff Deakin

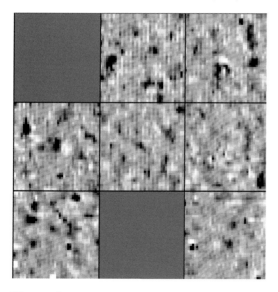

**Figure 4**

Although these results are similar to those produced by Mr Roger Ainslie (see figure 2, page 15), there appears to be two concentric ditches running from the middle right square into the top right square.

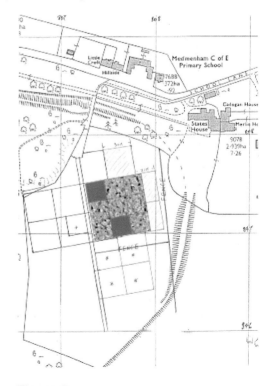

**Figure 5**

contours) of the Hill Fort. So, starting in August 2006, a series of 'training days' were held to acquaint AIM members and volunteers with the terrain, the features and the task before them.

The site was walked, photographs taken and particular features noted. The accuracy of the Ordnance Survey map was checked and the Ordnance Survey Bench Mark situated in the adjacent Bockmer Lane was eventually located.

In September, AIM members met again to confirm (or otherwise) the accuracy of a section of the banks and ditches, as previously recorded by the Ordnance Survey (OS). A couple of months later members gathered to measure and draw the feature (probably a quarry) in the middle-north area of the Hill Fort and to confirm (or otherwise) the accuracy of more of the banks and ditches, as recorded by the Ordnance Survey. All these features were mapped and recorded (see figure 6, page 18). The species of the trees and bushes covering the western part of the Hill Fort were also noted (see 'flora', page 4).

On two Sundays in March 2007, a small group braved the drizzle to record the westerly quarry area and to record a profile of the banks just south of the north-east corner of the Hill Fort, making use of the Bench Mark below. The initial profile was measured directly from the Bockmer Lane OS Bench Mark, at a right angle to the upper bank and then on the second Sunday a second profile was taken 130 metres south of the first (see figure 7, page 19).

In February 2008 a group of AIM members (see photograph 5 on page 19) gathered to receive training on the Total Station, bought with the grant money, to increase the quality and quantity of the surveying for the Project. The Total Station is an optical surveying instrument mounted on a tripod. It allows the operator to measure and store a series of heights, and/or distances and/or angles. The data is then downloaded on to a computer and the figures converted into contour, wire-frame and surface maps (for examples, see figures 9, 10 and 11 on pages 20 and 21). Using this instrument, the group surveyed a narrow strip of the north-west bank and ditch.

In late March 2008 and mid-April, a group of trainees met for a training day. In March the group worked with the Total Station to record two parallel lines laid out with 50 metre tapes across the north-west bank and ditch of the Hill Fort. To improve the results, in April, a larger section was targeted and four 50 metre tapes were laid out at right angles to the bank; these tapes were laid out two metres apart and measurements were recorded into the machine's memory, at two metre intervals along each tape (see figures 9, 10 and 11, pages 20 and 21).

The 'Training Day' held in late April 2008 also covered topographical surveying. It had been decided to survey a section of the bank that had mostly been ploughed out during the preceding millennia. So, the Total Station was erected and positioned on the eastern bank of the Hill Fort and its exact position was recorded (NGR SU80827:84691). Sixty-six readings were recorded across and along the bank (see figures 13, 14 and 15, pages 22 and 23).

# Medmenham Iron Age Hill Fort - Compilation site map, superimposed on the 1973 Ordnance Survey map, showing Resistivity and Magnetometry Results and all other investigatory work (North at top)

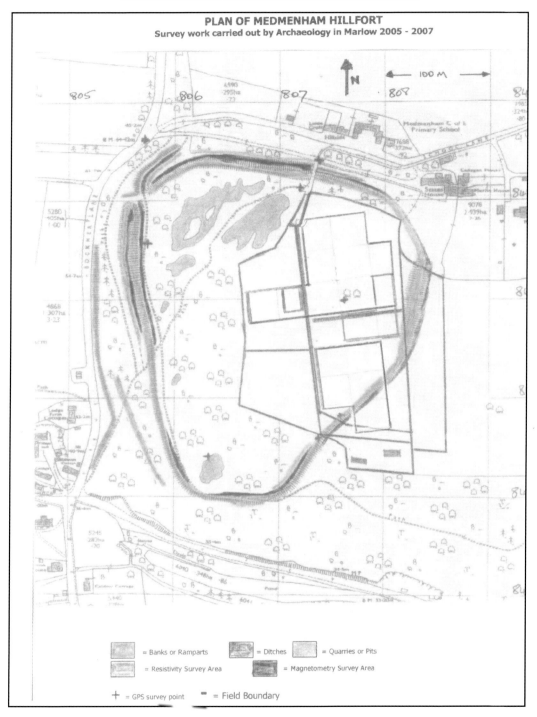

**Figure 6**  *(reproduced by permission of Ordnance Survey on behalf of HMSO. © Crown copyright 2005. All rights reserved. Ordnance Survey License number 100044133)*

## Medmenham Iron Age Hill Fort - Bank and ditch profiles measured and recorded in March 2007

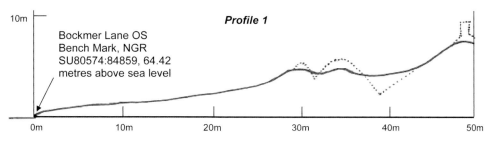

Profile 1 of the bank and ditch system of Medmenham Hill Fort runs north-west (0m) - south-east (40m). The additional dotted lines on the drawing give an indication of how the banks, ditches and a palisade may have looked when the fort was in use.

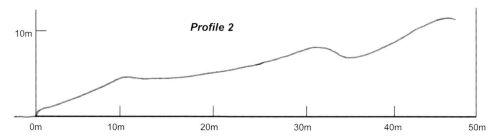

Profile 2 was taken 130 metres south of the OS Bench Mark and at this point the height above sea level was approximately 4 metres lower than the Bench Mark.

**Figure 7**

## Medmenham Iron Age Hill Fort - ROMADAM Training Day held in March 2008 to demonstrate the use of the Total Station surveying unit

**Photograph 5**

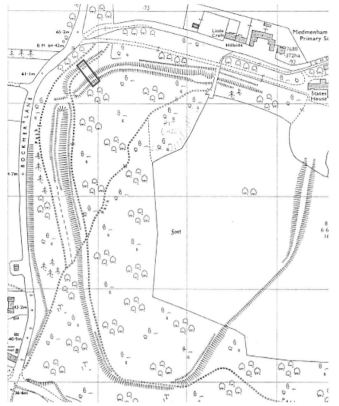

Map showing the area measured (in red rectangle), running from the south-east (crest of bank) north-west (bottom of slope).

**Figure 8**

**Surface Map**
Section below shows top bank in blue and secondary bank in mustard colour.

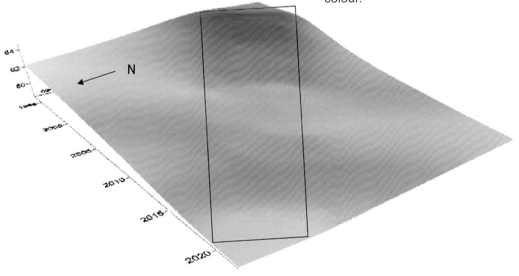

**Figure 9**

20

# Medmenham Iron Age Hill Fort - Results from Total Station Training Day in March 2008

**Wireframe Map**

Section showing top bank in blue and secondary bank in green/blue.

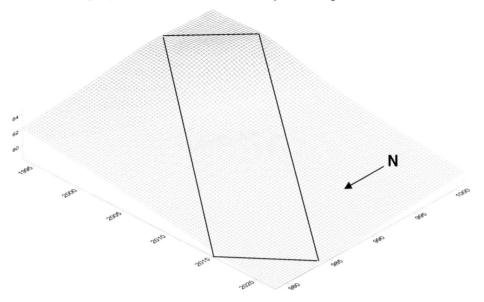

**Figure 10**

**Contour Map**

Bank shown (top left)

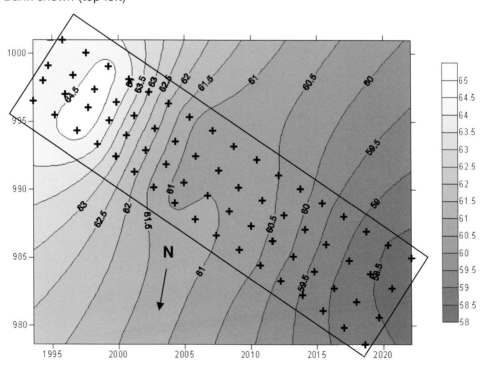

**Figure 11**

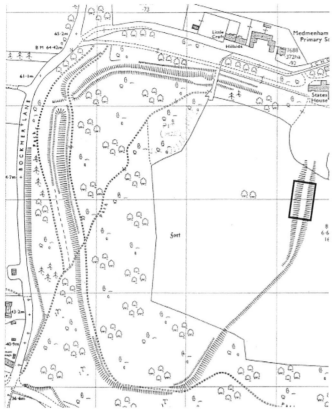

Map showing the area measured (in blue rectangle) and, below this, the resultant surface map.

**Figure 12**

**Surface Map**
Section between the lines shows the bank in blue, the slopes in light green.

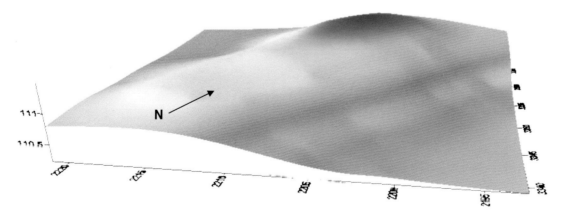

**Figure 13**

22

# Medmenham Iron Age Hill Fort - Results from Total Station Training Day in April 2008

## Wireframe Map
Section shows remaining bank in purple and its lower edges in green.

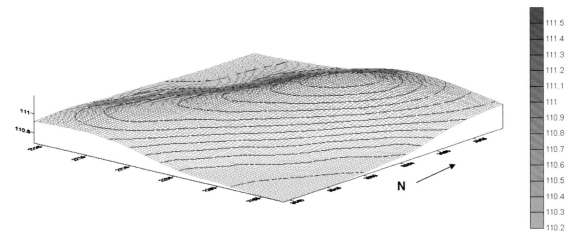

**Figure 14**

## Contour Map
Section showing part of the eastern bank.

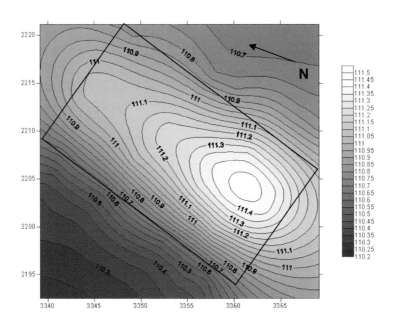

**Figure 15**

## 'The Keep' at Bolebec's Castle?

In March 2007, a group of AIM members assembled to try to try to discover the whereabouts of the 'keep' of Bolebec's Castle, as shown in Arthur Plaisted's book *The Romance of a Chiltern Village* (see map 6, page 25).

There is a triangle of land in the general area of the Plaisted map which, although sloping, slopes less than its surroundings. There is also a gully close by that might have been used as a track, or might be a gully formed by water running off the higher ground. If there was a keep with a well at its heart, it is not obvious now. The bank Plaisted drew does not seem to be visible today and there is no flat area to house a 'keep building', nor is there a damp, or wet area, or depression, which would indicate the presence of a well, or spring.

Unfortunately, although the 'training days' were great successes, no traces were found of any castle, nor its keep! There is, of course, a possibility that AIM was looking in the wrong places. If AIM ever has the time and funds to make a third investigation, it will.

## Global Positioning System (GPS), Laser Levels and Dowsing

In December 2007, Dr Tim Southern visited Medmenham Hill Fort to assist at the 'training day' aimed at understanding and using a Global Positioning System (GPS) and a Laser Level (see photograph 6, page 26).

13 people, consisting of AIM members, and other interested people, walked to the field next to the north-east field, where the remains of the Hill Fort bank are just visible. This area was chosen as it was free from trees. Mr Southern demonstrated his hand-held GPS unit, linked up to a vertical aerial (1.5 metres high), which gave a clearer signal than on its own. Although his unit gave fairly accurate measurements on a horizontal plane, its measurements of the vertical axis were not as accurate and could not be relied upon, as the actual differences in height in this area were minimal.

Mr Southern also demonstrated his laser level. The trainees took turns in taking 40 measurements from the staff, at half metre intervals along a 50 metre tape. The tape had been laid out to ensure that the full cross-section of the mostly ploughed out bank was accurately surveyed (see figures 16, 17 and 18, page 27).

The second part of the morning was devoted to dowsing. Two members of the Thames Valley Dowsers kindly demonstrated their techniques and reported that they had located a longish track running north-south in the north-east field, plus a curved feature (ditch?) near to the trees. Mr Southern and AIM members tried out the 'rods' and most experienced similar movements of the rods at the same spots as the Dowsers (see photograph 7, page 26).

In January 2008, 13 AIM members and Dowsers from Thames Valley Dowsers gathered for a 'training day' to learn about the use of dowsing in archaeology. At the south-east corner of the Hill Fort, the dowsers concentrated their efforts on the Norman.

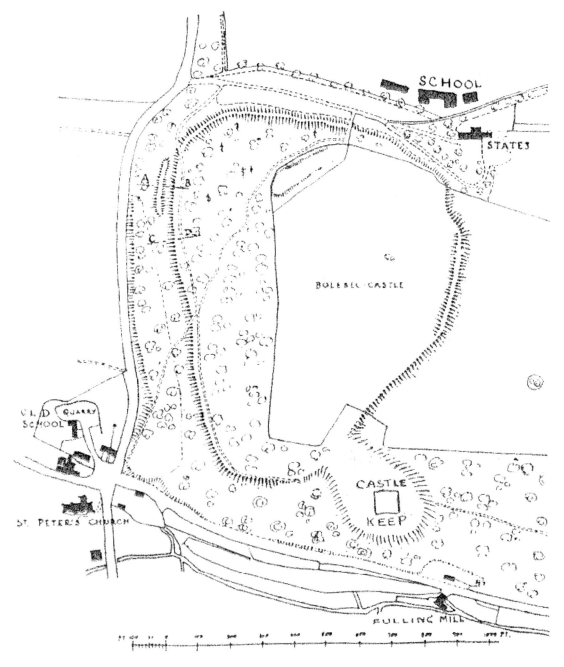

CAMP IN GILLMAN'S WOOD

**Map 6**

**Medmenham Iron Age Hill Fort - Dr Tim Southern at a ROMADAM Training Day in December 2007 demonstrating Global Positioning System (GPS) and Laser Level techniques - Lower photograph shows dowsing in operation**

**Photographs 6 and 7**

# Medmenham Iron Age Hill Fort - ROMADAM Training Day in December 2007 showing results from Laser Level measurements, NGR SU8085:8480

Profile shown in red, taken across eastern bank of the Hill Fort using Dr Southern's Laser Level; n.b. the figures in the profile in the bottom graphic run right to left, not left to right, and the vertical scale is exaggerated to emphasise the slope differentials.

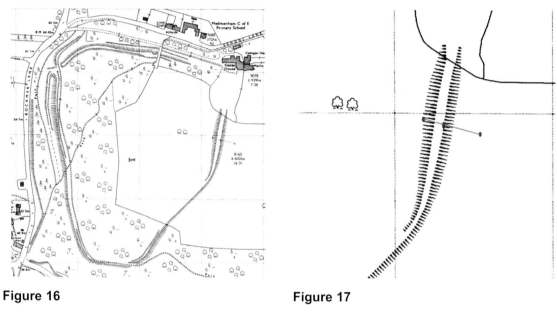

**Figure 16**                                    **Figure 17**

*(reproduced by permission of Ordnance Survey on Behalf of HMSO.©Crown copyright 2005. All rights reserved. Ordnance Survey License number 100044133)*

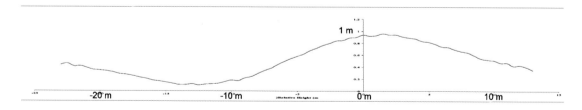

**Figure 18**

era. They believed an entrance and at least two water sources were located. The area investigated was a little east of where Plaisted had placed Bolebec's Castle's Keep on his map (see Map 6, page 25).

The dowsers were fairly certain that there were two castles (possibly castle and castle keep) within the local area. The group then visited the field to the east of the central track-way, running through the open area of the Hill Fort, where 30 metre squares had been laid out (as previously for magnetometry in 2005). The group began by trying to locate the Iron Age feature (possible Banjo Enclosure) as suggested by Mr Ainslie in 2005. With 13 people dowsing, a multitude of orange and yellow flags were inserted in five of the 30 metre squares. A series of concentric circles running around the single clump of trees became evident and were roughly transferred, by sight, on to a plan with the 30 metre squares already drawn upon it. Two tracks running slightly parallel and slightly east of the existing trackway were identified; the most easterly dividing into two towards the top of the field.  It is certainly possible that one of the dowsers' circles could have matched up with the Banjo Enclosure speculated by Mr Roger Ainslie (see figure 3, page 15) Due to time restrictions, we were unable to commence a specific search for Bolebec's Castle.

In late March 2008, another group of AIM members and members from the Thames Valley Dowsers (TVDs) met for a training day. In the north-east paddock, ranging poles had been positioned, as for previous investigations, in 30 metre square grids. Experienced and novice dowsers dowsed the field (see photograph 8, page 29) and the results, based on findings of a TVD member and an AIM member dowsing, were transferred to our base map by another TVD member (see figures 19 and 20, page 29). The dowsers' date of construction was 1132AD. Only excavation can verify these findings.

# Medmenham Iron Age Hill Fort - Results from 'Dowsing' Training Day held in March 2008, NGR SU8075:8465

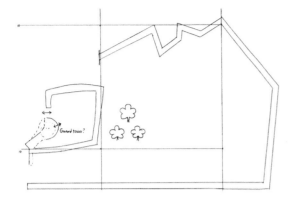

**Figure 19**

Dowsing results depicting an outline of a structure, also superimposed on site map. If Bolbec's Castle was constructed in wood, the Dowsers may have found it.

*(reproduced by permission of Ordnance Survey on Behalf of HMSO. © Crown copyright 2005. All rights reserved. Ordnance Survey License number 100044133)*

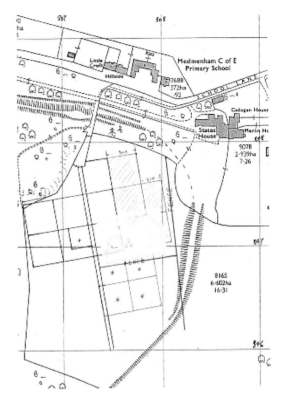

**Figure 20**

## Dowsers and AIM members at the Training Day

**Photograph 8**

## Conclusions

This site has probably been occupied for many thousands of years. The most significant and noticeable construction is the Hill Fort, which still remains a most impressive statement from our forefathers. Until an authorised excavation can be undertaken the exact date of construction can only be speculative. It is probably Iron Age (700BC to 43 AD), but its origins might be from the late Bronze Age (1000BC to 700BC).

The possible existence of a Banjo enclosure is interesting and, again, further authorised investigations may confirm its existence and its role within the landscape.

Although authors, writing in previous centuries, have stated the existence of Bolebec's Castle, scientific investigations failed to locate any trace. However, local dowsers detected the outline of a building in the area most likely to have housed a wooden castle (as stated by Plaisted in his 1958 book, 'castle built of timber not stone'). The keep of the castle is not discernible today, nor is a spring, or a well, but since over 900 years have passed since such a castle would have been built, the absence of such water features is not surprising.

Although now fairly overgrown, the evidence of quarrying for either gravel, clay and chalk, is still obvious today. Again minor authorised excavations should identify what resources were quarried and in what locations.

# Bibliography

Colmer F, *Memorials of Marlow*.

Editor - Ditchfield, 1901. *The Memorials of Old Buckinghamshire*. Bemrose and Son.

Pevsner, Nicholas, and Elizabeth Williamson, 1994. *Buckinghamshire. The Buildings of England*. London: Penguin Books.

Plaisted, Arthur H, 1925. *The Manor and Parish Records of Medmenham, Bucks. Medmenham*: The Village Bookshop.

Plaisted, Arthur H, 1958. *The Romance of a Chiltern Village – 5,000 BC to 1957 AD. Medmenham*: The Village Bookshop.

Roscoe, E. S, 1935. *Buckinghamshire Antiquities*. London: Methuen & Co. Ltd.,

Royal Commission on Historic Monuments (England), 1912. Buckinghamshire Vol. 1. HMSO.

Sites and Monuments Records (SMR) schedule, 1995. *Medmenham No 27140*.

St. Peter and St. Paul, Medmenham. Parish Church leaflet.

Underhill FM, 1959. *Letters to J. F. Head. 31 March 1951 and 11 September*. Sites and Monuments Records File, Aylesbury.

Victoria County History, 1925. *"Parishes: Medmenham". A History of the County of Buckingham: Volume 3.*

## Thanks and acknowledgements to

Archaeology In Marlow would like to thank Mr Roger Ainslie, Abingdon Archaeological Geophysics, 4 Sutton Close, Abingdon, Oxon, OX14 1ER, for his guidance, help and patience on the 24th March 2005, 22nd January & 26th February 2006; and Mr Geoffrey Deakin, who conducted two Magnetometry surveys in 2008.

AIM would also like to thank the landowners of the sections of land we were surveying, for giving their permissions for us to conduct our surveys.

AIM is extremely grateful that the Local Heritage Initiative (LHI) awarded the ROMADAM Project, (Recording Of Marlow And District's Ancient Monuments,) a grant (£22,605) to survey four earthwork sites close to Marlow. The money granted by LHI (now HLF) allowed these investigations to proceed.

English Heritage for their help and permissions
Mr Alex (Sandy) Kidd (Senior Archaeologist for Buckinghamshire) for his advice and help
Dr Tim Southern for his help on laser and GPS technologies
The Thames Valley Dowsers for dowsing explanations and demonstrations
Mr Ray Balkwell for cutting the long grass at Medmenham Hill Fort
Mr David Greenwood for his research work on Medmenham Hill Fort
Mr & Mrs Phillips for allowing us to have access to their land
Mr Shepherd for allowing us to have access to his land
Mr Cook for allowing us to have access to his land
Mr Hawes for allowing us to have access to his land
Mrs Moore for allowing us to have access to her land
AIM members, Dave Greenwood, Gerry Platten, Dave Axworthy, Ray Balkwell, Liz & Mike Miller, Mike & Sheila Hyde, Keith & Sally Bracey, Ann Pitwell, Eileen Bottjer, Brian Vallis, Julie Rushton, Robert Dunsmuir, Alison Meakes, Peter Ricketts, Andrew Wallace, Hazel Malpass and Tony Reeve
The many other members of AIM and members of the public who helped on the Project.

--------------

# Chapter Two

## *The First World War Training Trenches at Pullingshill Wood near Marlow Common*

The second ROMADAM (Recording of Marlow And District's Ancient Monuments) Project site to be investigated was the network of First World War Training Trenches dug in Pullingshill Wood, one mile west of Marlow Town, Buckinghamshire. These trenches are well known to Marlow people, and the area within the parts of Pullingshill Wood and Marlow Common are known locally as 'The Trenches'. National Grid Reference SU8216:8630.

### Proposal

Mr Mike Hyde, the Secretary of the Marlow Museum Project, had encouraged Archaeology in Marlow (AIM) to investigate and record the Trenches and, being a member of both the Woodland Trust, the owners of the site, and AIM, made the initial approaches to the Woodland Trust on AIM's behalf.

As there appeared to be no record of the plan, or layout, of these trenches, the AIM proposal to the Lottery Heritage Initiative (LHI) consisted of conducting research into the origins of the 'Trenches', surveying the area and then producing a detailed plan, showing the results, before natural and other changes in the ground format removed most, if not all, of the traces of this important part of the local and national history. Permission was sought and received from the Woodland Trust to plot their topography and record their presence within the landscape, as long as no excavations took place.

Also, AIM was entrusted to produce a leaflet describing the research and outcomes of the work and to use this information to produce two display panels to be placed in the vicinity of the trenches, for the benefit of the people from Marlow and Medmenham and visitors to the area. In addition AIM would pass the results of the survey to the Woodland Trust, English Heritage, English Nature, the Archaeology Department at Bucks County Council and the Army Regiments who were likely to have been involved in the 'Trenches'.

### Purpose and Usage

The Training Trenches were constructed during the early stages of World War 1 (1915) as part of the training for the troops who were about to depart for the war in Europe and beyond.

### Location

This large network of trenches, on a high part of the Chiltern hills, within the Chilterns Area of Outstanding Natural Beauty, is situated wholly within Pullingshill Wood. Pullingshill Wood is the property of the Woodland Trust and situated slightly west of a minor road which runs from the A4155, Marlow to Henley road, to the Bovingdon Green - Frieth road. See map 7 and aerial photograph 9 on page 34 and map 8 on page 35, for the exact location.

# Location of First World War Training Trenches

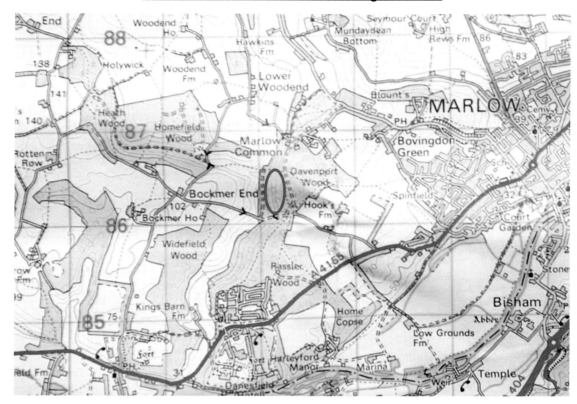

**Map 7**   *(reprodued by permission of Ordnance Survey on Behalf of HMSO. © Crown copyright 2005. All rights reserved. Ordnance Survey License number 100044133)*

## Aerial photograph of First World War Training Trenches taken in 1945

A few trench outlines can be seen on the left 'bottle shaped' area of the photograph opposite.

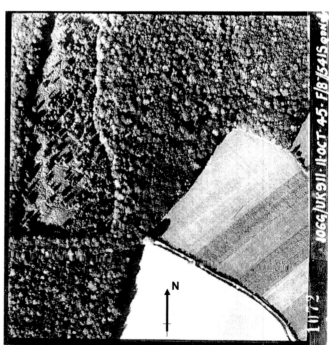

Aerial photograph 11-10-1945 (106/G/UK911) reproduced with permission of English Heritage (NMR) RAF photography

**Photograph 9**

# 1960 Ordnance Survey Map, 6 inches to 1 mile, showing Pullingshill Wood in the centre with Homefield Wood opposite

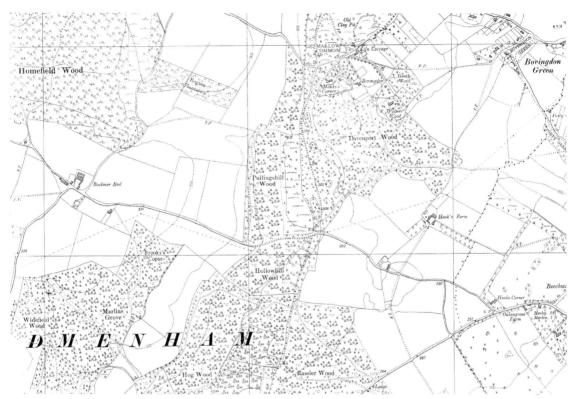

Map 8     *(reproduced by permission of Ordnance Survey on Behalf of HMSO.© Crown copyright 2005. All rights reserved. Ordnance Survey License number 100044133)*

## Topography, Geology and Flora

The trenches extend over an area measuring 360 metres by 100 metres (approximately 3.5 hectares) and overlook a gently sloping valley. The trenches are about 90 metres above sea level and the valley floor is about 60 metres above sea level. Homefield Wood can be observed on the opposite side of the valley at a similar height to the trenches. The trenches were cut into a plateau of 'older river gravel' lying over 'upper chalk' bedrock. When the trenches were originally dug, the area they occupied was probably cleared of most vegetation. During the last 90 years the heathland has reverted to woodland, with bracken and bramble covering much of it (see photographs 10 and 11 on page 37). The predominant tree is the silver birch, with oak, beech and sweet chestnut present and a few scots pines and ash, which probably grow as a result of natural seeding from trees in the surrounding woods. Within the woods are ancient banks, which probably marked the parish boundaries, and also pits, which are evidence of chalk, flint and clay workings.

## Research

Discussions took place between AIM and authorities, such as, the MOD (Defence Estates), Thames Valley Western Front Association and the Imperial War Museum, to try and gather relevant information. All the local newspapers of the period, held in the local library, were also reviewed and then references to such military bodies who may have been involved during this work were followed up e.g. the Grenadier Guards, the Royal Engineers, the 3/5th London Field Ambulance, etc.

Following Britain's entry into The First World War on August 4th 1914, hundreds of thousands of volunteers joined the forces and were then billeted, or encamped, close to, or in, various towns and cities for training, before going on active service.

The South Bucks Free Press newspaper printed the following accounts of activities in and around Marlow.

- 27/11/1914 - ". ….large numbers of troops arrive in High Wycombe. . . billeted from one end of town to the other... including large numbers at Dawes Hill Park."

- Jan-Mar 1915 - Marlow Urban District Council receives complaints that in spite of large numbers of local men volunteering for the war, the town is not being accorded the privilege of hosting troops such as Wycombe, Maidenhead, Slough, etc. They enlist the aid of General Sir George Higginson, one of Marlow's most distinguished residents, ex-Brigade of Guards (see photograph 12, page 39).

- 17/5/1915 - Brigade of Guards confirm that they have now agreed to send 1200 troops of the 3rd Battalion Grenadier Guards and 800 men of the 4th Battalion to be housed under canvas at Bovingdon Green (see photographs 16 and 17, page 39).

- 4/6/1915 - The 3rd Battalion under Colonel Corry arrive at Bovingdon Green camp. A YMCA tent is set up to provide refreshment to the troops under the leadership of Miss Dorothy Light of the Vicarage at Marlow.

**A view of a small part of the Trenches network in Pullingshill Wood in 2008**

**Mr David Greenwood of AIM talking about the Trenches to visitors from the Chiltern Historic Environment - Woodland Seminar, in March 2006**

**Photographs 10 & 11**

- 18/6/1915 - Arrival of the 4th Battalion and very significantly "During the week the men have been kept busily employed with their training. The range at Quarry Woods has been used for firing parties nearly every morning and <u>trench digging</u> and field exercises have been carried out in the woods to the north of the town."

- 21/6/1915 - Gen. Higginson's 89th birthday held at his home, Gyldernscroft, with a full battalion of 1100 men marching to join him for celebrations (see photograph 14, page 39).

- 23/7/1915 - The 3rd Battalion go off on active service; various other troops arrive, particularly RAMC (21/7/1915); rifle training continues at Cock Marsh and Quarry Wood; various sports days during the summer. The 5th Battalion Grenadier Guards is being formed at this time.

- 20/8/1915 - The Prince of Wales drives over from Windsor to inspect the troops.

- 10/9/1915 – Another company of the 5th Battalion Grenadier Guards arrives at Bovingdon Green camp, followed by a reserve battalion of the Welsh Guards, who use the Cock Marsh range at Bourne End.

- 15/10/1915 - Grenadier Guards leaving camp in Marlow, followed by the Welsh Guards two days later. The 26th Royal Fusiliers (Bankers) arrive on the 17th at the camp (they leave around 20/11/1915).

- 19/11/1915 - Heavy gales blow down most tents and finally close Bovingdon Camp. The 3/5th London Field Ambulance and the Bankers Battalion were billeted in buildings and various empty houses in Marlow.

- 22/12/1915 – RAMC troops (3/5th London Field Ambulance) leave Marlow.

- 24/12/1915 - Arrival in the district of 2000 Royal Engineers, part of the Eastern Division. Three field companies are billeted in Marlow, others in west, east and north Maidenhead and in Cookham.

- 1/3/1916 - Heavy snow, major flooding, gales, trees down. Royal Engineers help in the rescue effort.

All summer long there were reports of sports and social activities, including football matches and concerts (see photographs 18 and 19, page 39). Significant numbers of the Royal Engineers were sent off on active duty in August 1916.

In addition to the above newspaper reports, Wing Commander Derek Martin (then a resident of Medmenham) remembers chatting to a local man named Charlie Colison who informed W/C Martin that he (and presumably other men) helped to dig (at least some of) the trenches at Pullingshill Wood.

# Photographs taken in 1915

12. General Higginson

13. Troops marching through Marlow

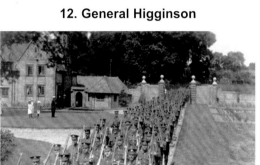

14. Troops arriving at Glyndernscroft

15. Troops marching past the Royal Oak

16. Troops arriving on Bovingdon Green

17. Camp at Bovingdon Green

18. Sports Day at Bovingdon Green

19. Sports Day at Bovingdon Green

Above photographs reproduced courtesy of Marlow Town Council and others

## Method and Implementation

The task before AIM was both vast and difficult and it was essential that an efficient and accurate method was established before embarking on a complete survey of the site. It is also an essential part of any LHI project to involve as many local people as possible and to offer training at every level.

To this end Mr Mike Farley (Archaeological Consultant and previous Buckinghamshire County Archaeologist) was invited to visit the trenches in April 2005. Mr Farley explained the benefits and shortcomings of various different approaches that could be adopted to achieve the objective. Mr Farley also advised AIM what equipment would be needed and the publications which could be helpful (see photographs 20 and 21 on page 41).

As a result of Mr Farley's visit and his advice, a 'training day' was held in May 2005 to try out some of Mr Farley's recommendations to see which might work best. It was decided that a base line should be established running roughly north-south through the centre of the trench network. It is necessary to have fixed points when surveying or mapping a site, so either a fixed Ordnance Survey (OS) bench mark, or a series of temporary bench marks (TBMs), is needed. As no OS bench marks were nearby, six TBMs were inserted along the base line using metal pegs embedded in concrete plugs and their positions were recorded using a global positioning system (GPS). This base line was then used to lay out evaluation squares, set at right-angles, on both sides of the base line.

AIM decided to survey the whole site by marking out 20 metre squares. Measurements were then taken at one metre intervals, using tape measures parallel to the baseline, within each 20 metre square. Where the tape crossed a trench edge a reading was recorded on to a record sheet and then on to graph paper, marked out with a scaled 20 metre square. Although recording readings from sixty-two 20-metre squares resulted in AIM producing a very large plan, reductions in scale by photocopying, allowed presentation of a manageable document.

These readings showed only where a significant change in the ground level occurred. AIM decided that it was not within the scope of its work to show where subtle changes in height occurred. Thus the final drawings depicted the current plan of the trench network.

## The Surveying

From July to November 2005 over 20 people helped with the measuring of the Trenches. 16 visits were made, in order to survey every one of the 62 squares, 8 of which were found to be devoid of trench activity.

## Results

On page 42 there is a plan (figure 21) showing the networks of all the training trenches at Pullingshill Wood. Figure 22 (page 42) superimposes the networks on to the local area map.

**Volunteers reconnoitring the Trenches in Pullingshill Wood in January 2005**

**Mr Mike Farley (extreme left), advising volunteers on the options available to survey the Trenches successfully, in Pullingshill Wood in April 2005**

**Photographs 20 & 21**

## Pullingshill Wood First World War Training Trenches 2005
## Plan showing Temporary Bench Marks (TBMs), NGR SU8216:8630

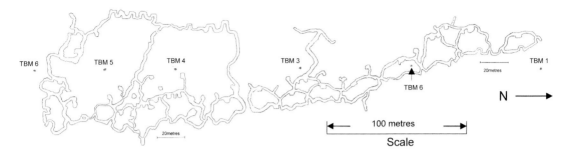

**Figure 21**

## Pullingshill Wood First World War Training Trenches - 2005 Trench Plan
## superimposed on local map (North at top) see Map 7, page 34, for exact location

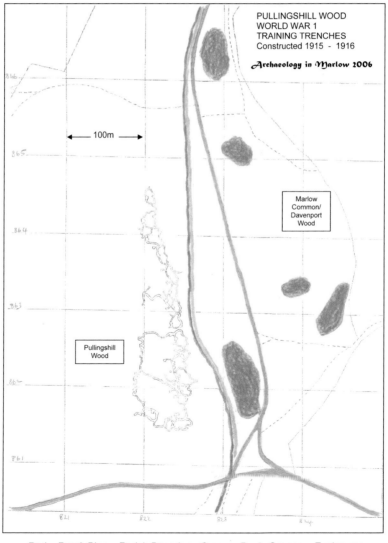

**Figure 22**      *Red = Road, Blue = Parish Boundary, Green = Bank, Orange = Enclosures*

A few notes of explanation of trench construction and use may be useful to interested readers. Research has shown that trenches were generally dug to about 7 feet deep and 6 feet wide, although we do not yet know whether the Marlow Trenches were dug to this, or any other typical design. We also know that trenches on the Western Front were often dug in three rows. The 'front line', 'the support line' and the 'reserve, or rear line'. Usually 'communications' trenches fed forwards from the rear line, but usually at an angle (not a right angle).

The front trench had a front bank (parapet) and a rear bank (parados) that was slightly higher. Both banks had around 75cms of sandbags on top of them and there had to be a 'fire step' dug into the front bank so that soldiers were positioned high enough to fire at the enemy. The trench bottoms were generally lined with 'duck boards' in order to avoid muddy and putrid conditions that could lead to medical problems, such as 'trench foot'.

The front line trench was often dug in a crenellated fashion (trench direction continually offset), so that attacking troops could not fire down a long straight trench. The front parts were called 'fire bays' and the offset parts, running parallel, but a couple of meters back, were called 'traverses'. Sometimes 'saps' were dug 30 metres, or so, into 'no man's land' as 'listening posts'. 'Sap' comes from 'Zappa', Italian for spade (used to approach, or undermine the enemy in siege warfare) – hence the word 'sapper' for an army engineer!

Trenches were designed to have 'machine gun nests', 'strong points' and had to have passing places for obvious reasons.

AIM is indebted to Mr Martin Brown (MOD Archaeologist) and Dr Danny Dawson (M.A. thesis) for their interpretations of how the trenches functioned all those years ago (see figure 23, page 44 and figure 24, page 45). Readers will observe that Mr Brown's interpretation has 'the enemy' to the west at Homefield Wood (see map 8, page 35) and Dr Dawson has 'the enemy' in the east.

Following the completion of this part of the ROMADAM Project, Mr Hyde wrote a detailed article, which was published in the Woodland Trust's magazine, Broadleaf,

**Profile Measurements**

It is quite likely that the trenches on Marlow Common looked considerably different in 1915 from how they look now, since they were probably deeper and had much steeper sides. The sides of the trenches, as we see them now, are considerably eroded and the bases are slowly filling with a layer of leaves and leaf-mould. The following set of cross-sections were recorded at eight positions within the trenches (see figure 25, page 46) and show two of these current profiles (see figure 26, page 46).

## Pullingshill Wood First World War Training Trenches - 2005, an interpretation by Martin Brown (Archaeologist for the MOD)

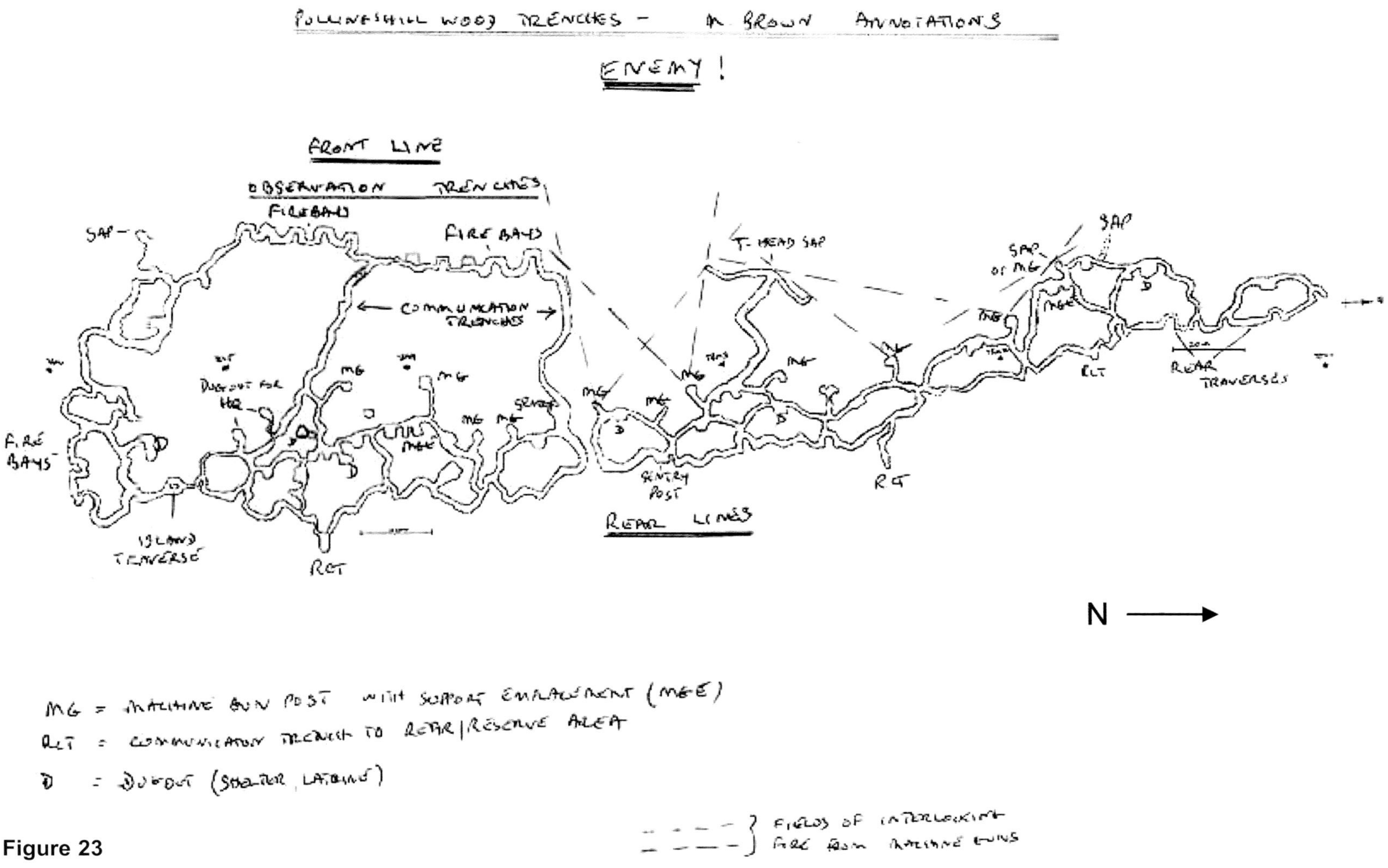

**Figure 23**

## Pullingshill Wood First World War Training Trenches - 2005,
## An Interpretation by Dr Danny Dawson

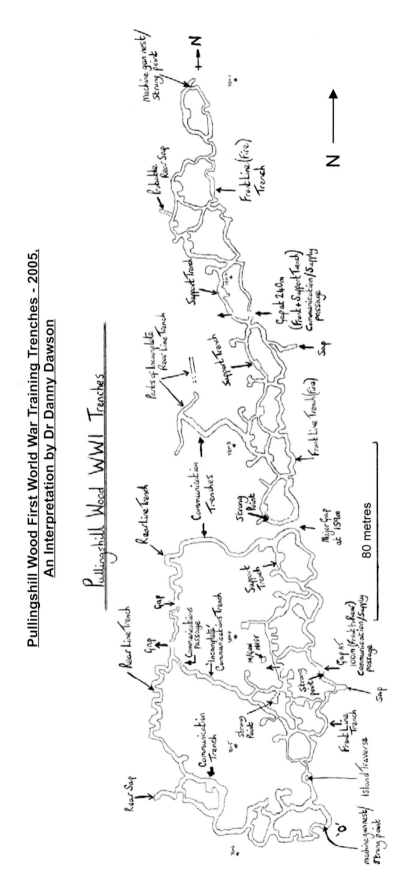

Pullingshill Wood WWI Trenches

Machine gun nest / Strong point

Probable Rear Sap

Front Line (Fire) Trench

Support Trench

Gap at 240m (Front & Support Trench) Communication/Supply passage

Sap

Patches of Incomplete Rear Line Trench

Support Trench

Front Line Trench (Fire)

Strong Point

Major Gap at 150m

80 metres

Rear Line Trench

Reactive Trench

Communication Trenches

Support Trench

Communications Passage

Incomplete Communications Trench

M/gun Nest

Strong Point

Gap at 100m (Front to Rear) Communication/Supply passage

Sap

Rear Line Trench

Gap

Gap

Communication Trench

Strong Point

Front Line Trench

Rear Sap

Communication Trench

Island Traverse

'O'

machine gun nest / Strong point

N

Figure 24

## Pullingshill Wood First World War Training Trenches - 2005
## showing profiles S1 and N2 (Figure 26) and locations of all profiles taken

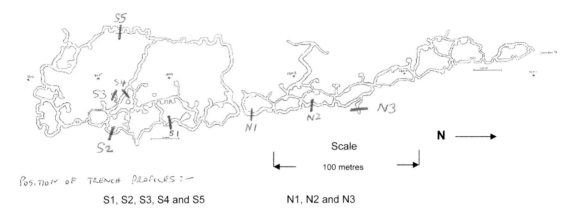

POSITION OF TRENCH PROFILES :-

S1, S2, S3, S4 and S5          N1, N2 and N3

**Figure 25**

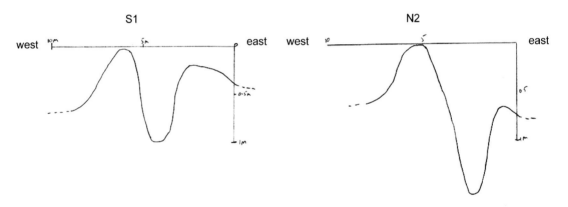

**Figure 26**

## Conclusions

AIM, having carried out the research and physical investigations, now knows considerably more about the 'Trenches'. It is known which regiments of troops were involved in the digging, by whom they were led and that local people were also involved. Many of the events were photographed. A detailed drawing of the trenches, which are in fact in two distinctly different parts, has been produced, giving a permanent record. This is important since, as the whole area is in open woodland, it is gradually being eroded and disappearing. The Woodland Trust, together with the County Archaeological Service, is considering how best this area can be preserved. It is one of the best and most complete examples of World War 1 Training Trenches left in the country and really ought to be preserved, especially as a memorial to the men who trained there. Information panels have been installed to give more information about the area to visitors.

## Unveiling of one of the two Permanent Information Boards

In the early morning of Monday the 24th of September 2007 the wind was blowing and the rain was sheeting down. However, when an invited group of interested people assembled at 10.30am at Pullingshill Wood the sky was blue and the sun shone through the autumn leaves.

From the photograph 22 on page 48, it can be seen that, despite the earlier weather, there was a good turnout. Amongst the guests were Mr Sandy Kidd (Senior Archaeologist for Bucks), Mr Loren Eldred of The Woodland Trust, Mr John Morris of The Chiltern Woodland Project and a good selection of AIM members.

John Laker (Vice-Chairman of AIM) welcomed everyone and then gave a short speech thanking The Woodland Trust and English Nature for allowing AIM to conduct the survey of the First World War Training Trenches. The Woodland Trust arranged for the installation of the information boards and helped to transfer AIM's design into a reality.

Mr Laker then expressed AIM's gratitude to The Local Heritage Initiative for providing the grant which enabled AIM to conduct this part of the ROMADAM Project. He also thanked Dave Greenwood, who energetically drove the project forward, and the many other AIM members and local volunteers who helped with the surveying and compilation of research needed to record the site and its history as accurately as possible. AIM surveyed sixty-two squares each measuring 20m x 20m in 2005, from July to November  -  more than 24,000 readings!

AIM were fortunate to have three Parish Council Chairmen to help with the proceedings. Councillor Mr Richard Scott (Mayor of Marlow) led the group in a minute's silence to honour those who trained at the trenches in preparation for the fighting on the Western Front. The Chairman of Medmenham Parish Council (and AIM Member), Mrs Helen Balkwell, spoke next, mentioning her childhood memories of playing in the trenches. The Chairman of Great Marlow Parish Council, Mrs Janet Pritchard, spoke of living in close proximity to the trenches and her Welsh parentage (one of the Regiments trained was the Welsh Guards).

Glasses were raised in remembrance of the men who trained in the trenches, many of whom subsequently did not return from foreign fields. Mrs Pritchard then unveiled one of the impressive permanent information boards.

Those present then had the chance to see the board and all the information recorded on it.

**Pullingshill Wood First World War Training Trenches**
**2007 - Information Board unveiling**

**Photograph 22**

Unveiling of one of the Pullingshill Information Boards on Monday 24th September 2007 (AIM members and invited guests, including Mrs Janet Pritchard, Marlow Rural Parish Council Chairman (front middle), Mrs Helen Balkwell, Medmenham Parish Council Chairman (front right), and Mr Richard Scott, Marlow Town Mayor (front left).

## Suggested Reading

- M Brown: A Mirror of the Apocalypse (Great War Training Trenches) in MOD Sanctuary magazine no 33, 2004
- M Brown: Journey back to Hell (Excavations on the Somme) in Current World Archaeology magazine no 10, 2005
- P Griffith: Fortifications of the Western Front 1914 – 1918, Osprey 2004
- War Office: British Trench Warfare 1917 – 1918, Imperial War museum 1997
- F Ponsonby: Grenadier Guards in the Great War 1914 – 1918, MacMillan 1920

## Other Training Trench Sites

- Berkhamstead Common, Herts
- Whiteleaf Hill, Bucks
- Sheffield, South Yorkshire
- Penally, Pembrokeshire
- Otterburn, Northumberland
- Seaford Head, East Sussex
- Salisbury Plain, Wiltshire

## Bibliography

Dawson, D, 2007. *"A Better 'Ole: A Study of 20th Century Military Landscape in Buckinghamshire."* unpublished thesis.
South Bucks Free Press, Various Cuttings from 1915.

## Thanks and acknowledgements to

Archaeology in Marlow is extremely grateful that the Local Heritage Initiative (LHI) awarded the ROMADAM Project, a grant to survey four earthwork sites close to Marlow, which allowed these investigations to proceed.

English Heritage for their help and permissions
English Nature for their help and permission
The Woodland Trust for their help and permission
Marlow Town Council for their permission to reproduce their photographs
Sandy Kidd (Senior Archaeologist for Buckinghamshire) for his advice and help
Mike Farley for his advice and consultation work at Pullingshill Wood
Mike Hyde (Marlow Museum Project Secretary and Woodland Trust member) for his encouragement and his invaluable liaison work
Wing Commander Martin for his help and research
Martin Brown (MOD) for his interpretation of the plan of the Trenches
Dr Danny Dawson for his interpretation of the plan of the Trenches
David Axworthy for his research work on the Trenches

AIM members, Dave Greenwood, Gerry Platten, Dave Axworthy, Ray Balkwell, Liz & Mike Miller, Keith & Sally Bracey, Ann Pitwell, Peter Ricketts, Andrew Wallace, Sarah Duxbury, Mike Hyde and Sylvia Paton
The many other members of AIM and members of the public who helped on the Project

And lastly to all the men who trained in the Trenches, but did not return.

--------------

# Chapter Three

## *An Earthwork in Warren Wood, off Winchbottom Lane, Little Marlow*

The third ROMADAM Project monument to be investigated was the roughly circular earthwork of uncertain age at Little Marlow, east of Marlow town; National Grid Reference - SU8715:8972

### Proposal

As the age and purpose of this banked enclosure was in doubt, AIM decided to investigate the man-made construction to see if its age and purpose could be identified. The AIM proposal to the Local Heritage Initiative (LHI) was to carry out research, to survey the earthwork and to produce a detailed plan, so that a permanent record could be made.

Also, AIM was entrusted to use this information to produce a display panel to be placed to the side of the footpath, close to the earthwork, for the benefit of local people and visitors to the area. AIM was also committed to produce a leaflet describing the research and outcomes of the work. In addition AIM would pass the results of their investigations to the owners of the site, English Heritage and the Archaeology Department at Bucks County Council.

### Purpose & Usage

The purpose and usage of the earthwork was mostly unknown and apart from a very good hachure* drawing made by Mr Arthur Boarder, there has been no detailed survey conducted of the earthwork. *hachures look a bit like flat-headed tadpoles - the head depicting the highest point and the tail depicting the lowest point.*

### Location

Sometimes footpaths lead walkers to interesting places and the footpath to Warren Wood is no exception. If visitors leave Marlow on the A4155, travelling towards Bourne End, then cross the bypass and take the next left turn after the garden centre, Winchbottom Lane, about a mile up the lane they will find a footpath on the right; this leads up to Warren Wood, but it is a very steep climb! A short distance after the gradient of the footpath has levelled out, the man-made earthwork can easily be seen to the left of the AIM information board. See maps 9 and 10 on page 52 and map 11 on page 54, for the exact location.

### Topography, Geology and Flora

Situated on the chalk hills of the Chilterns, the earthwork measures approximately 50 metres in diameter and is approximately 100 metres above sea level. The earthwork was constructed on a plateau of glacial sand and gravel deposited by a previous ice age, which lies over the chalk bedrock. There is a good sprinkling of trees: beech, sessile oak, ash and holly predominate, along with a liberal covering of brambles and ferns (see photograph 23, page 54).

# Location of Warren Wood Earthwork

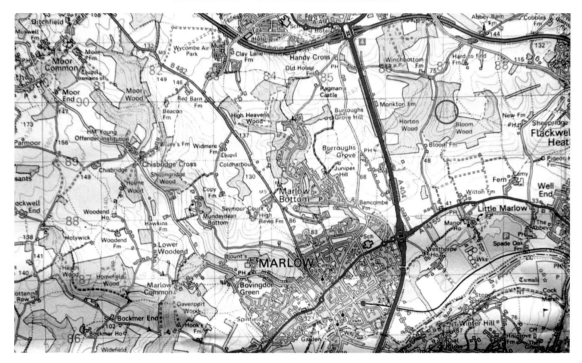

**Map 9** *(reproduced by permission of Ordnance Survey on Behalf of HMSO. © Crown copyright 2005. All rights reserved. Ordnance Survey License number 100044133)*

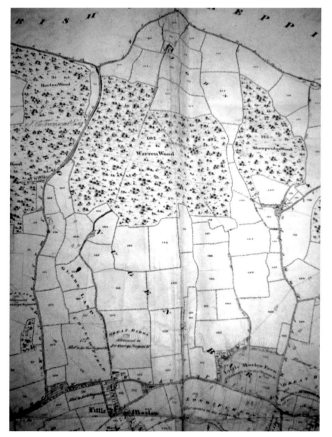

An extract from 'the Little Marlow Inclosure Map' of 1821, showing Warren Wood, reproduced with the kind permission of The Centre for Buckinghamshire Studies in Aylesbury.

**Map 10**

# Research

- The oldest maps available show Warren Wood as a wood. Unfortunately, the Domesday Book does not tell us whether, or not, the area was a wood in 1086, although Little Marlow was assessed for 50 pigs, suggesting the area must have had some woodlands.

- Although the earthwork has existed within Warren Wood, Little Marlow, for a considerable time, its first appearance is on a 1993 Ordnance Survey (OS) Pathfinder Map (see map 11 on page 54). Apart from the Inclosure map of 1821 (see map 10, page 52), the next instance of either Warren Wood, or the adjacent Bloom Wood, being named on a map is on Bryant's 1825 map (it states 'Broom Wood', but has no mention of Warren Wood). Broom Wood is also shown on Lipscomb's 1847 map. Warren Wood is first mentioned on the 1870 OS map and Bloom Wood, rather than Broom Wood, first appears on the 1883 OS map.

- The significance of Broom Wood rather than Bloom Wood, is that Bloom might indicate the presence of past iron working (a 'bloom' is a ball of molten metal, usually iron). However, the name Broom Wood is unlikely to have the same connotations.

- Investigations had previously taken place on the site by Mr David Wilson (a member of Maidenhead Archaeological and Historical Society) and Mr Roger Carter, both in 1975, and by Mr Arthur Boarder in 1978 (an amateur archaeologist and Marlow man).

- Mr Wilson is reported to have found a rim of a pot of very coarse greyware in the bank and a lump of grey clay and some red tiles. He thought that the pottery sherd, or piece, might have been 13th Century (greyware was produced in the 13th and 14th centuries).

- Also in 1975 Mr Boarder made notes of a visit by Mr Carter in July of that year. These notes included the discovery of 'two flint and mortar masses – walls', as well as, 'a base and a body sherd (a piece of the body of the pot) of sandy grey unglazed pottery' and 'pieces of peg tile' (tiles were probably made locally at Lane End, or Penn, both in Bucks).

- In 1978 Mr Boarder wrote his own report, which included a more detailed sketch of the southern enclosure (see figure 27, page 55) on which a small section of 'flint wall' is drawn, running north - south, adjacent to its northern side, none of which is apparent today. Mr Boarder collected pieces of tile and pottery which he thought were medieval. He believed the pottery was similar to that found at Fillington Wood, a medieval earthwork (late 13th to 14th century) and at other local sites. Although AIM made comprehensive and extensive efforts to locate both sets of Warren Wood pottery sherds, none of these have been located, so far, but Mr Boarder took a photograph of the pottery sherds he found (see photograph 24, page 56).

## Ordnance Survey Map, 2½ inches to 1 mile showing Earthwork at Warren Wood

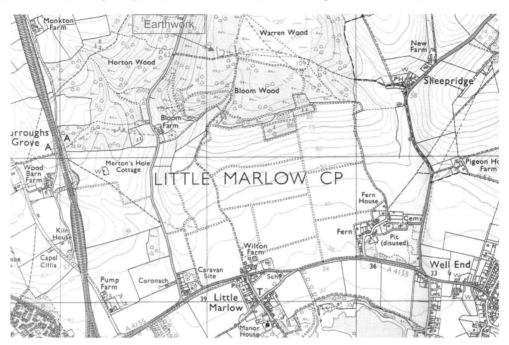

**Map 11**    *(reproduced by permission of Ordnance Survey on Behalf of HMSO. © Crown copyright 2005. All rights reserved. Ordnance Survey License number 100044133)*

## Bank and ditch of the inner enclosure at Warren Wood, close to the public footpath

**Photograph 23**

## Hachure Drawing of inner enclosure of Warren Wood made by Arthur Boarder in 1978

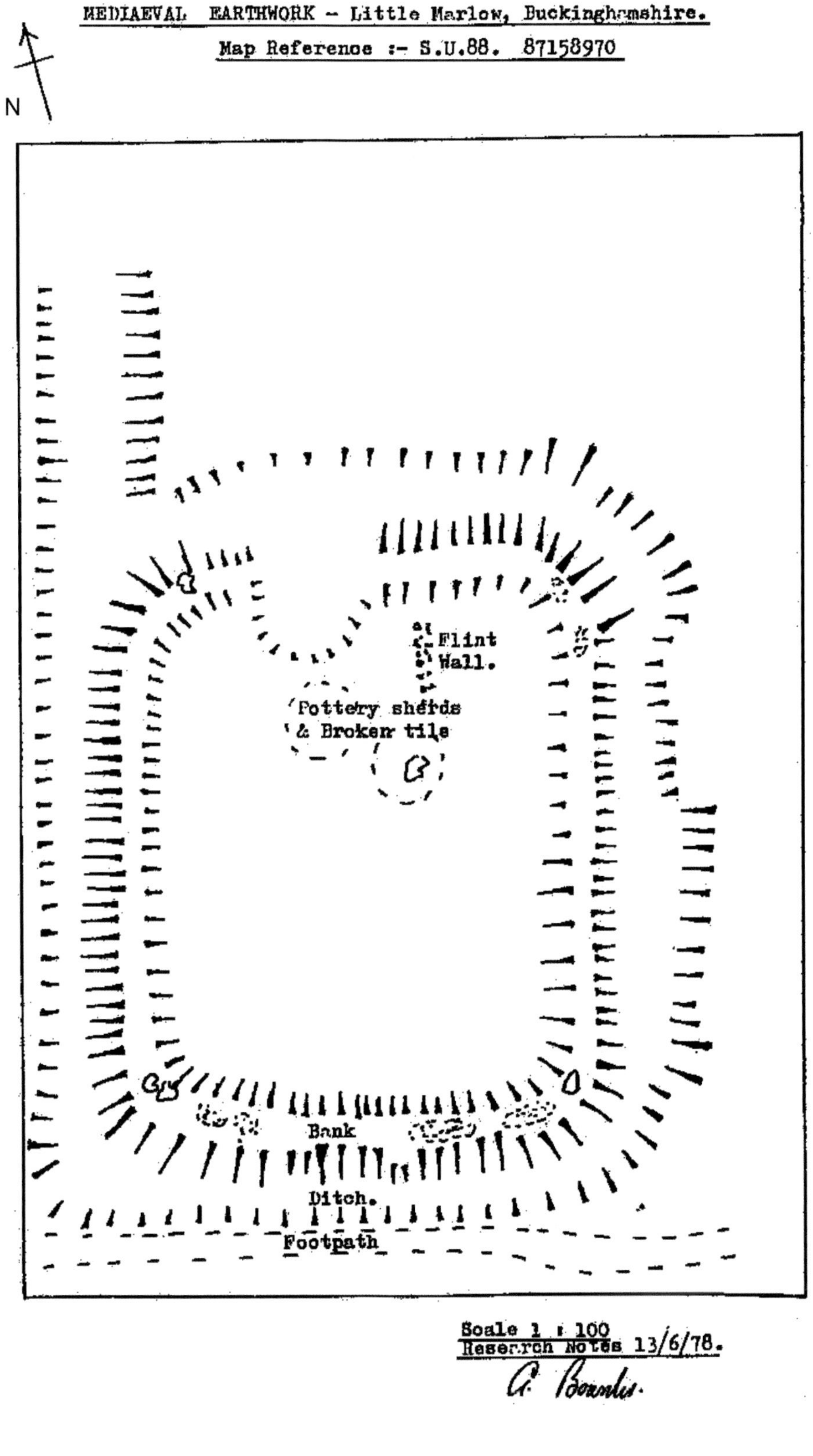

MEDIAEVAL EARTHWORK - Little Marlow, Buckinghamshire.
Map Reference :- S.U.88. 87158970
N
Flint Wall.
Pottery sherds & Broken tile
Bank
Ditch.
Footpath
Scale 1 : 100
Research Notes 13/6/78.
A. Boarder.


Figure 27

## Photograph taken by Arthur Boarder of pottery sherds found in inner enclosure of Warren Wood in 1978

**Photograph 24**

- A comprehensive work by Mr Andrew Pike entitled Earthwork Enclosures in the Buckinghamshire Chilterns lists six other earthwork enclosures, along with three more possibilities.

The drawing below (figure 28) is taken from Mr Pike's study and shows an earthwork in Brays Wood, The Lee, Bucks.

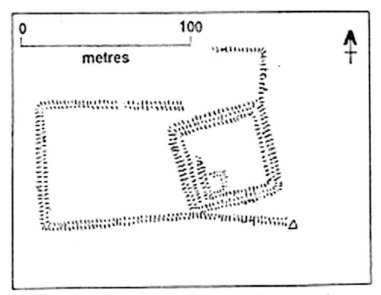

Fig. 46. No. 1 The Lee (Brays Wood). After Allcroft 1908, 473.

**Figure 28**

Mr Pike writes

*The average size and shape of these enclosures resemble a largish moat about 150m x 75m. None has been excavated and their function must remain conjectural.*

*All the enclosures lack documentary evidence. In contrast, the relatively few moated sites in the Chilterns can usually be equated with known manors, as recorded in the Victoria County History – Buckinghamshire publication, in the relevant parish. This suggests that the enclosures did not have an administrative function but that the banks and ditches had some sort of defensive purpose rather than the mainly "decorative" status of moats. Many of the enclosures contain subsidiary enclosures either within the principal one or alongside it, suggesting a house site. Interestingly, at least three of the enclosures have produced iron slag, indicating industrial activity. All the enclosures are situated in woodland; this may account for their survival, but it also points to some form of activity associated with the famous Chiltern Beechwoods. One possibility is that the enclosures were connected with the chase and that they contained dwellings used as hunting lodges, or lived in by game-keepers.*

*In short, these enclosures can perhaps be interpreted as the centres of small woodland settlements, with the principal dwelling and outbuildings situated within the smaller enclosure, where there is one. The larger "bailey enclosure" would have, perhaps, afforded protection to a small domestic herd from wild animals, such as deer and wild boar, which were prevalent in Buckinghamshire in the medieval period. It would doubtless be the deer and boar, which were the principal animals that were hunted. Fieldwork in some of the enclosures has produced small quantities of medieval pottery so, despite the lack of documentary evidence, a date in the medieval period for these structures may be suggested.*

- Other similar sites outside the Chilterns exist at Sarratt (Marginia Wick) in Hertfordshire, in the New Forest, south of Gaze Hill, in Hampshire (a possible swine pound) and at Chobham Common on the Bagshot Sands in Surrey (pigs might have been kept there, as their chief food was the mast of fallen beech and oak).

- The maximum dimensions of the inner and outer enclosures at Warren Wood taken together are 96 metres (north to south) and 74 metres (east to west) and appears to be roughly average size.

## Method and Implementation

The task before AIM was relatively difficult and it was essential that an efficient and accurate method was established before embarking upon a complete survey of the site. An essential part of any LHI project is to involve as many local people as possible and to offer training at every level.

After much discussion, it was decided to establish a 'base line' running roughly east-west, to the north of the earthwork. The base line was to be a length of twine linking two Temporary Bench Marks (TBMs). A 'Bench Mark' is a known spot, usually recorded by the Ordnance Survey, but as the nearest OS Bench Mark was some considerable distance away, the two TBMs were installed and their positions recorded using Global Positioning System (GPS) equipment.

The TBMs had metal pegs embedded in concrete bases and were inserted in the earth at each end of this line. The metal pegs protruded above the ground and AIM's vertical measuring staff was always placed on these pegs first, so that a 'base height, or 'elevation' could be established. All subsequent readings were adjusted from the 'base height'. The base line ran between the pegs and, once established, had tapes run from it at 90 degrees at one metre intervals. Vertical measurements were then taken along the tapes at one metre intervals, using the level and the staff.

# The Survey

During November 2005, six volunteers visited Warren Wood to survey the site. A length of twine was strung between the two TBMs and a Dumpy Level was set up (a Dumpy Level consists of an optical instrument, or telescope, mounted upon a tripod. The horizontal plane of the telescope is adjusted until it is level; readings can then be taken from the staff). The heights of the two TBMs were measured and surprisingly they were recorded at identical elevations. A clever device, known as an 'optical square', which employs mirrors to establish a right angle, was used to create one at a distance of 5 metres along the base line (row 1) and measurements, from the staff, were taken at one metre intervals along 'row 1'. These measurements were recorded on sheets, which allowed five rows to be recorded on one sheet.

Between November 2005 and April 2006, the site was visited eleven times and a total of 59 rows were surveyed (see photographs 25 and 26 on page 60). All the readings that AIM had recorded were transferred on to an Excel spreadsheet and forwarded to Oxford Archaeology who kindly converted the data into two graphics (see figure 29, page 61)

In September 2006, AIM invited Mr Mike Farley (of Michael Farley Archaeology) to visit the site. Mr Farley noticed that a bank extended from the north-west corner of the earthwork in a straight line, then turned right (east) and ran in a straight line again, then turned right again (south) and joined the earthwork again at the north-east corner. The bank had a shallow ditch on its outside. This new banked enclosure had a less prominent bank than the one we had already surveyed. It is possible that this extension was an outer enclosure for keeping livestock, or possibly wild animals, or game birds for hunting purposes. If this view is correct, the original enclosure AIM surveyed might have been an enclosure for the habitation of a person, or, possibly, a family.

The tile fragments and pottery sherds identified by Mr Boarder in 1978 as medieval (see photograph 24, page 56) might also indicate the earthwork had a building within its confines at some time in the past.

In January 2007, seven volunteers (five AIM members & two local people) gathered at the site to take measurements of the outer enclosure that Mr Farley had identified, with the intention of transferring them to a 'hachure drawing' which would show the inner and outer enclosures.

To achieve this, 100 metre lines were laid out (using two 50 metre tapes) at 90 degrees to the north of the original base line, using the Optical Square. Measurements were then taken at right angles from the tape at 5 metre intervals. Three measurements were taken at each of these 5 metre intervals - the edge of the inner ditch, the summit of the bank and the edge of the outer ditch.

These readings were entered directly on to an A3 graph paper drawing, which already had the inner enclosure, converted into a hachure drawing, at one end. A few days later, using tracing paper, the new readings were converted into hachures and a composite drawing produced (see figure 30, page 62).

## Some of the AIM members and local people who helped to survey Warren Wood Earthworks

## Dumpy Level being used to survey Warren Wood Earthworks

**Photographs 25 and 26**

## Warren Wood
## Plan and Isometric Projection of the Inner Enclosure

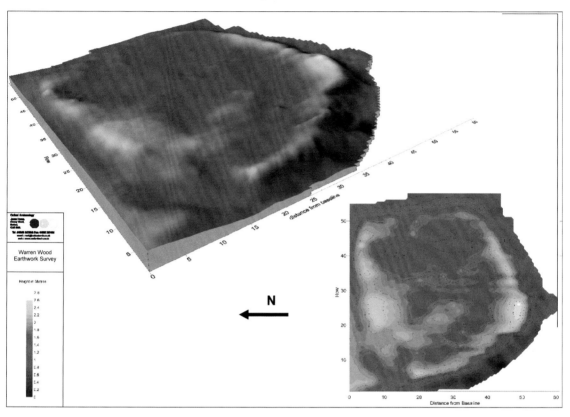

*Graphic produced for Archaeology In Marlow by Oxford Archaeology Unit Ltd. ©*

Yellowish colours depict the higher points (bank) and the brownish colours depict the lower points (internal plateau and outer ditch).

The figures in the graphic are in metres. The '0m' to '60m' line 'distance from baseline' runs approximately north ('0m') - south ('60m').

**Figure 29**

# Warren Wood
## Hachured Graphic showing inner and outer enclosures

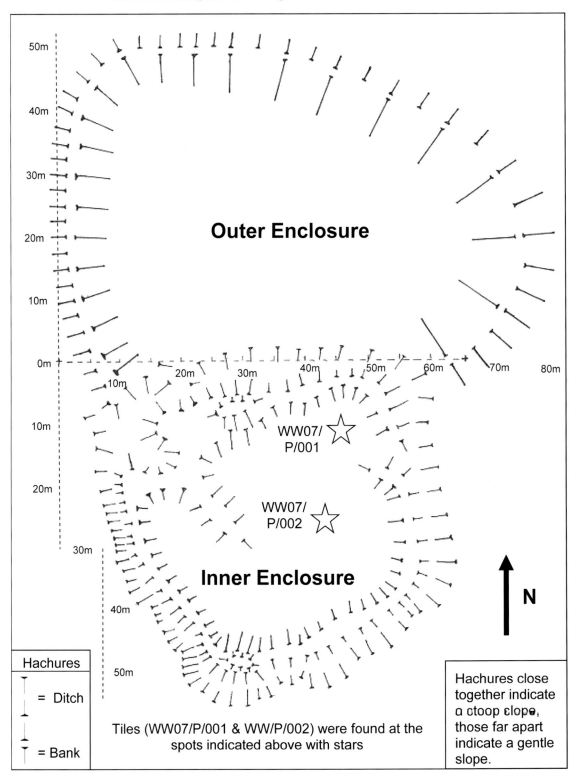

Tiles (WW07/P/001 & WW/P/002) were found at the spots indicated above with stars

**Hachures**

| | |
|---|---|
| ⊤ = Ditch | |
| ⊥ = Bank | |

Hachures close together indicate a ctoop clope, those far apart indicate a gentle slope.

**Figure 30**

In November 2007, another visit took place and a combination of ranging poles and a builder's level were used to ascertain the differences in height between banks and ditches. The southern and western sides of the earthwork had differentials, between the top of the bank and the base of the ditch, of between 1.6 metres and 2.2 metres (south-west corner). In other places, no differential was obvious, but these might be either ancient, or relatively modern, access points.

As the searches for the pottery sherds found by previous archaeologists (see photograph 24, page 56) had proved fruitless, it was decided to fieldwalk both the inner and outer enclosures to try to locate any remaining pottery sherds. Unfortunately, no sherds were found. However, two pieces of tile (probably roof) were found, recorded as small finds (artefacts), plotted on to the site drawing and then removed temporarily from the site for possible dating (see figure 30, page 62 and following spreadsheets). Unfortunately, the two roof tile pieces could not be accurately dated, as the style runs across three, or four, centuries.

**Pottery/Ceramic Building Materials (CBM) Items found in Inner Enclosure**

| No. | Description | Weight in grams | Comments |
|---|---|---|---|
| WW07/P/001 | Tile | 220 | Orange/black sandwich |
| WW07/P/002 | Tile | 270 | Orange/black sandwich |

AIM also invited two local metal detectorists to the site in the hope that artefacts (coins), might be found, which may have given a date of habitation. Unfortunately, only modern artefacts were found. A 10p and 50p coin were unearthed (not recorded), plus two unidentified pieces of metal and eleven cartridge cases. These items (except the two modern coins) were recorded on 'small find' sheets, but due to their relative unimportance, were not plotted on the site drawing.

**Metallic Items found in Inner and Outer Enclosures**

| No. | Description | Weight in grams | Comments |
|---|---|---|---|
| WW07/M/001 | Piece of Metal | 15 | Probably waste material |
| WW07/M/002 | Chunk of Metal | 25 | Probably waste material |
| WW07/M/003 | Cartridge cases (11) | 105 (total) | 0.303" (Relatively Modern) |

AIM then assembled all the survey information and combined it into one comprehensive graphic to be used on the Information Board installed at Warren Wood (see figure 30, page 62).

## Unveiling of the Information Board

At the end of February 2008, the Warren Wood Information Panel was unveiled by Little Marlow Parish Council Chairman, Mr Dallas Banfield, in the company of Messrs Richard and Anthony Mash (the owners of Warren Wood) and a group of AIM members and local people, all braving the inhospitable weather (see photograph 27 on page 64). The information board is sited alongside the footpath, close to the earthwork, for the benefit of visitors from Little Marlow and beyond.

## Installation of Information Board at Warren Wood on 29th February 2008

**Photograph 27**

## Conclusion

The site is probably medieval and a gamekeeper, stockman, or swineherd, probably lived in, or used, a building in the inner enclosure, possibly as a family home. The inner enclosure may have been used to keep domestic, or wild, animals initially, and the outer enclosure may have then been constructed as the main enclosure.

It is likely that either, pigs, or milking cows, were kept commercially, or possibly wild boar, or wild deer, were corralled in the outer enclosure for hunting purposes.

## Continuing work

AIM hopes to conduct more investigations at Warren Wood in years to come, so that knowledge of this ancient and interesting site can be expanded.

## Bibliography

Boarder AWF, 1975. *Notes from visit to Warren Wood by Roger Carter* - not published, but at Sites and Monuments Record (SMR) Aylesbury.
Boarder AWF and Carter RF, 1978. *Research Notes - Medieval Site in Warren Wood*, not published, but at SMR Aylesbury.
British Geological Survey, 1996. *London and the Thames Valley*.
*Domesday Book,* 2002. *A Complete Translation*, Dr A Williams & Prof GH Martin.
Gardiner E, (MB [Cantab] FSA), 1924. *A Triple Banked Enclosure on Chobham Common*, Surrey
Hampshire County Council, 1981. *Hampshire Treasures, Volume 5 (New Forest).* Archeological Collections, Vol 35,
Hertfordshire County Council, 2004. *Historic Environment Record - Earthwork Marginia Wick, Sarratt*, Reference - HER 0885
Lipscomb, George, 1847. *The Hundred of Desborough, Bucks*, History and Antiquities of the County of Bucks, Vol 3.
Parker & Boarder, 1969-74. *Fillington Wood Investigations.*
Parker RF and Boarder AWF, 1991, *A medieval settlement at Fillington Wood, West Wycombe*. Records of Bucks 33.
Pike A, 1995. *Earthwork Enclosures in the Buckinghamshire Chilterns* - Chiltern Archaeology: Recent work.
Secker D, 2005. *A survey of earthworks and structural remains at Bray's Wood, The Lee.* Records of Bucks 45.
Sites and Monuments Record, 2006. *Earthwork at Bloom Wood, Little Marlow. SMR No. CAS 1176.* Buckinghamshire County Council,
Victoria County History, 1925. *A History of Buckinghamshire III.*
Wilson D, 1975. *Notes from investigation* - not published, but at SMR Aylesbury.

**Thanks and acknowledgements to**

Archaeology in Marlow is extremely grateful to the Local Heritage Initiative (LHI) who awarded the ROMADAM Project, (Recording Of Marlow And District's Ancient Monuments) a grant of £22,605 to survey four earthwork sites close to Marlow.

The Local Heritage Initiative for Funding the ROMADAM Project
Messrs A and R Mash for allowing us to have access to their land
Mr Alex (Sandy) Kidd (Senior Archaeologist for Buckinghamshire) for his advice and help
Mr Mike Farley for his advice and consultation work at Warren Wood
Oxford Archaeology for their advice and for producing the Warren Wood graphic
Mr Arthur Boarder for providing his 1978 report, his notes, his advice and his photograph
Mr David Wilson for his advice and use of the notes from his 1975 investigation
Mr Trevor Bownass for lending AIM his Dumpy Level and staff
Mr David Axworthy for his research work on Warren Wood
Metal Detectorists Mr Eddie Mitchell and Mr John Bird
AIM members, Dave Greenwood, Gerry Platten, Dave Axworthy, Ray Balkwell, Liz & Mike Miller, Ann Pitwell, Peter Ricketts, Andrew Wallace, Mike Hyde, John Laker and the Ford family,
The many other members of AIM and members of the public who helped on the Project.

---------------

# Chapter Four

## *The Iron Age Hill Fort at Danesfield*

The fourth ROMADAM Project monument to be investigated was the Iron Age Hill Fort at Danesfield, west of Marlow; National Grid Reference SU8176:8440.

### Proposal

Although plans had previously been drawn of the Iron Age Hill Fort at Danesfield and subsequently published, AIM wanted to conduct a topographic survey in order to produce an accurate plan of the features that are still present on this site. So, AIM applied for and received a grant from the Local Heritage Initiative (LHI) to carry out research and to survey the Hill Fort.

The AIM proposal to LHI consisted of gathering research into the Hill Fort, surveying the site and then producing a detailed plan, showing the results. Also, AIM were entrusted to produce a leaflet describing the research and outcomes of the work and to use this information to produce a display panel (or panels) to be placed close to the Hill Fort, for the benefit of the employees of SAS UK, employees and guests of the Danesfield House Hotel and Spa. Interested visitors must liaise with either, or both, companies to gain access to the Hill Fort. In addition AIM would pass the results of the investigations to the two owners of the site, English Heritage and the Archaeology Department at Bucks County Council.

### Location

See Map 12 on page 68, for the exact location.

About 2 kilometres west of Marlow, going towards Henley on the A4155, is a roundabout. The left exit leads to SAS UK's headquarters (see photograph 28, page 69). A further half a mile down the A4155 road to Henley is the entrance to Danesfield Hotel and Spa (see photograph 29, page 69). Wholly within the properties owned by these two companies are the remains of a Hill Fort. The Hill Fort is only accessible with the agreement of the owners and is a Scheduled Monument (no. 27156) under the protection of English Heritage.

### Purpose & Usage

As mentioned in chapter one, some Hill Forts were used to store grain in numerous underground pits, others were probably used to keep cattle and/or sheep safe from rival tribes, others contain evidence of structures indicating protected settlements and some were possibly used as high status residences of tribal chiefs and their families.

The Danesfield Hill Fort again lies within the area occupied by the Catuvellauni tribe, or people. The tribe occupying the south side of the Thames, opposite Danesfield, was the Atrebates.

## Location of Danesfield Iron Age Hill Fort

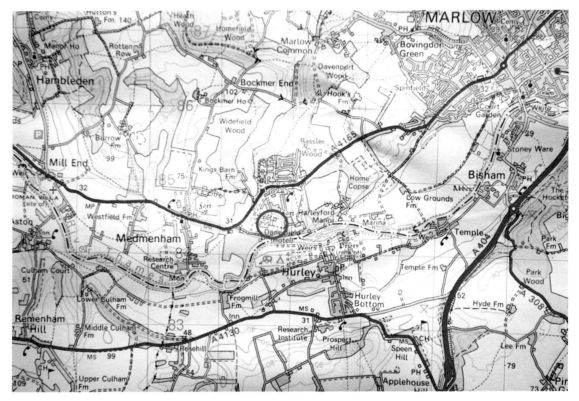

**Map 12**    *(reproduced by permission of Ordnance Survey on Behalf of HMSO. © Crown copyright 2005. All rights reserved. Ordnance Survey License number 100044133)*

## Headquarters of SAS UK Ltd

## Danesfield House Hotel and Spa

**Photographs 28 and 29**

## Topography, Geology and Flora

The Hill Fort at Danesfield is roughly 'horse-shoe shaped' and is most likely to have been constructed by Iron Age people somewhere between 2,000 and 2,700 years ago. Unfortunately, approximately a quarter of the Hill Fort was removed when the second Danesfield House was built (see 'Research' below) and the present hotel complex lies across the western section of the Hill Fort (see maps 13 and 14 on page 71). The eastern and northern banks and ditches of the Hill Fort are on SAS UK's land and have a good covering of trees and undergrowth. The southern side of the Hill Fort's defences is completed by a chalk cliff which towers above the River Thames below. The southern section has a spring which flows into a valley which runs down to the Thames and this area, owned by the Hotel complex, is known as 'The Cascades'.

The Hill Fort is positioned on a plateau occupying about 6.5 hectares and is around 60 to 75 metres above sea level and approximately 35 metres higher than the edge of the River Thames's flood plain below.

The geology of this prehistoric site dates from various ice ages over the last 500,000 years where generally 'older river' gravel is found lying over 'upper chalk' bedrock.

Although the centre of the Hill Fort has fewer trees, there is a diverse selection on and around the Hill Fort's banks, with field maple, silver birch, box, hazel, beech, ash, holly, pedunculate oak, elder, sycamore and yew; also buddleia and rhododendron have been introduced. Where there is undergrowth, it consists of ferns, stinging nettles and brambles (see photographs 30 and 31 on page 72).

There is barely a kilometre between Danesfield Iron Age Hill Fort and its western neighbour, Medmenham Iron Age Hill Fort, which is also known as Gillman's Camp, or Wood.

## Research into Historical Records and Previous Investigations

- Buildings probably existed nearby in the early 18th century, including Medlicotts Farm, and this building, or buildings, were probably extended, or redeveloped by John Morton in the early 1750s to form the first Danesfield House. This house was about 200 metres north of the present Danesfield Hotel and was outside the confines of the Hill Fort. In the mid-nineteenth century, a Roman Catholic Chapel, designed by Augustus Pugin, was built to the north of the house (see Map 13 on page 71). A further example of a Pugin design is North Lodge (previously Danesfield Lodge) built in 1844, which is on the left just before entering SAS UK's main gates. Between 1898 and 1901 a new Danesfield House was built by Robert Hudson of Hudson soaps to replace the first one which was demolished along with the Chapel (see Map 14, page 71).

- In 1797, in Thomas Langley's, *The History & Antiquities of the Hundred of Desborough*, 'In the grounds of Robert Scott esq., there is a strong and perfect Danish encampment in the form of a rude horse-shoe. In its circular part it is fortified by a double vallum; the front towards the Thames is defended by a high cliff'.

# The 1895 Sale map, showing the original Danesfield House

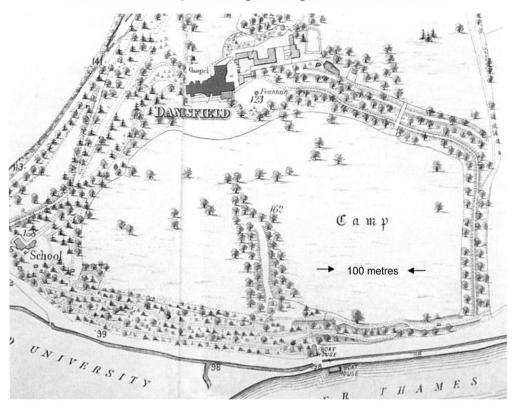

**Map 13**      An extract from 'the 1895 Sale map', reproduced with kind permission of The Centre for Buckinghamshire Studies in Aylesbury

# Ordnance Survey Map of 1925, showing the site of the new Danesfield House

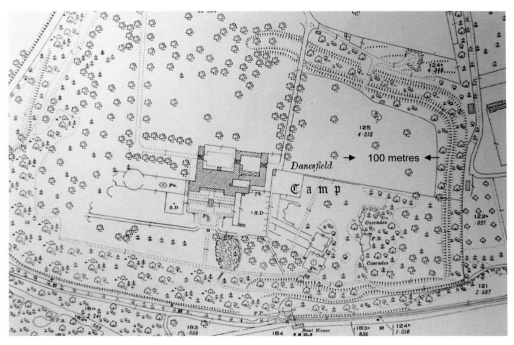

**Map 14**

# Danesfield Iron Age Hill Fort - Ditches and banks on north side

**Photographs 30 and 31**

- In 1911, AH Cocks reports a bronze spearhead having been found on 20th of July 1901 when the new Danesfield House was being constructed. Interestingly, he says in his *The Danes' Ditches at Danesfield (Medmenham)*, "Lipscomb confuses the earthwork here, known as the Danes' Ditches with the 'strong mounds or embankments in a wood above Medmenham church', which surround the reputed site of Bolebec's Castle, but they are ½ a mile away". There is a detailed drawing of the remains of the earthwork after the Danesfield House construction.

- The Hill Fort is again mentioned in 1912 by the *Royal Commission for Historic Monuments (RCHM) Vol 1*. 'Camp, known as Dane's Ditches, is situated at Danesfield ¾m east of church on north bank of river Thames. The work which formerly covered approximately 20 acres is interesting not-with-standing its incomplete state, on account of its form and position. The defences consist, on the N and E of a ditch with inner rampart and outer bank. The rampart at its strongest point is 17.5 ft high and 63ft wide; the ditch is 12.5 ft deep and 70ft wide'.

- In 1925, the Reverend Arthur Plaisted reported in his book, *The Manor & Parish records of Medmenham*, stating, 'The promontory fort is distinguished by simplicity of plan, economy of labour, and the absence of any discernable provision for the herding of animals'. Plaisted also compares Danesfield with Dyke Mills in Dorchester (on Thames).

- In 1951, a letter in *Sites and Monuments Records (SMR) file*: Mr F M Underhill to Mr J F Head 31/3/51: 'The Danesfield entrenchment is more prominent than the Gillman's Wood camp, and covers a spur of chalk in a loop of the Thames. The bank and ditch are extremely well preserved on the northern and eastern side. The western side is now gone, the north-western corner having been destroyed in the 18th century for the building of the 1st Danesfield mansion'.

- In 1958 Plaisted wrote in his book, *The Romance of a Chiltern Village*, that, 'Material from the fosse was piled along the valla, to form a bank crowned with a stockade. The ditches were not continuous, but segments were left where the solid earth has apparently remained undisturbed; a peculiar feature which has given them the name Causeway Camps'.

- From 1941 until 1977 the site, including Danesfield House, were taken over by the RAF. During World War II, RAF Medmenham was home to the Allied Central Interpretation Unit, which printed and collated aerial photographs taken from Spitfires and Mosquito planes whilst flying over enemy territory and seaways. This surveillance work, establishing what the enemy was doing and where it was being done, was crucial to the Allies' war efforts.

- Prior to the vacation of the site in 1994, the site housed the headquarters of the Ministry of Defence Police Training School (see map 15 on page 75).

- In 1982, 3 Neolithic/Bronze Age flint flakes were found during an excavation conducted by Michael Farley of Michael Farley Archaeology, but no features were recorded.

- In 1990 and 1997, Oxford Archaeology conducted investigations prior to extensions to Danesfield House being built. In 1990, evaluation trenches and test pits were dug by Keevill & Campbell, who unearthed many items of worked flint and pottery and these were dated from Neolithic (New Stone Age, 4,400 to 2,200BC) to Iron Age (700BC to 43AD). They unearthed a Mesolithic (Middle Stone Age, 10,000 to 4,400BC) flint, Iron Age pottery sherds (pieces of pottery, usually small), some dating from the 3rd century BC, grains of spelt wheat, barley and oats and even wattle/daub (used to make walls, made from interwoven sticks and mud mixture). In addition, they identified evidence of buildings within the Hill Fort. The Hill Fort was dated to the middle Iron Age (about 2350BC). The artefacts found can be viewed at the Buckinghamshire Museum site at Halton, by appointment. The 'accession number' is 1993.46. The 1997 investigation's test pits did not reveal any archaeology.

- In 1996, *The Sites and Monuments Record (SMR) schedule, Danesfield No 27156*, records that excavations in 1990 had 'uncovered shallow ditches, post-holes and pits containing Middle and Late Iron Age pottery, and the remains of a post-built structure with daub walls. Still earlier activity was demonstrated by the discovery of 71 flint artefacts, several of which provided the dating evidence for a shallow gully. These finds confirmed that the promontory had been inhabited in the Neolithic or early Bronze Age'

- In 1998, Northampton Archaeology conducted an investigation for SAS UK. They found scattered Iron Age pits and ditches - a total of four ditches, three pits and a possible post hole. Approximately 30 sherds of Iron Age pottery were found in various trenches, indicating sporadic activity in the Iron Age.

- Between 2003 and 2005, AIM investigated a construction thought to be an 'Ice-house', on SAS's property, near the west edge of the embankments (on further investigation it was identified as a structure for storing water). Whilst excavating around the structure, an excellent example of a worked flint was found. This flint and all the other artefacts found were given back to SAS UK with a copy of the AIM report.

## Danesfield Iron Age Hill Fort - Ordnance Survey Map 1:2500 showing RAF Medmenham buildings complex constructed during World War II

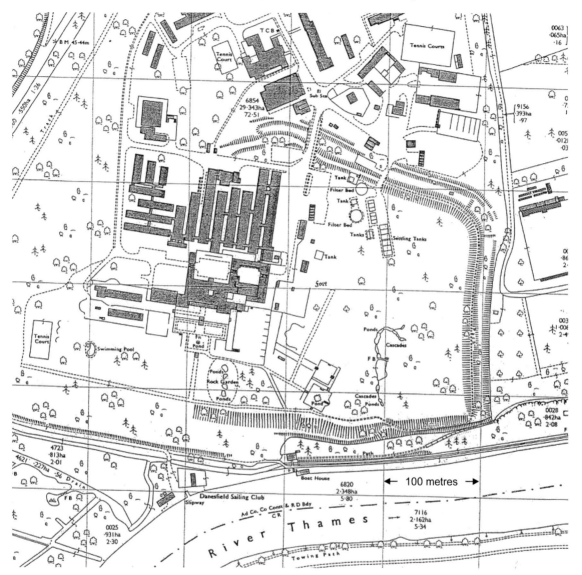

**Map 15**     *(reproduced by permission of Ordnance Survey on Behalf of HMSO. © Crown copyright 2005. All rights reserved. Ordnance Survey License number 100044133)*

## Method and Implementation

In April 2007 seven volunteers visited the Iron Age Hill Fort at Danesfield. As the Hill Fort is partitioned by a chainlink fence, the visit started at the northern and eastern sections, owned by SAS UK, and then the volunteers drove around to the Danesfield Hotel and Spa Centre to see the southern and western sides.

The northern part of the Hill Fort consists of two banks with a substantial ditch between

# Danesfield Iron Age Hill Fort - Showing banks and ditches

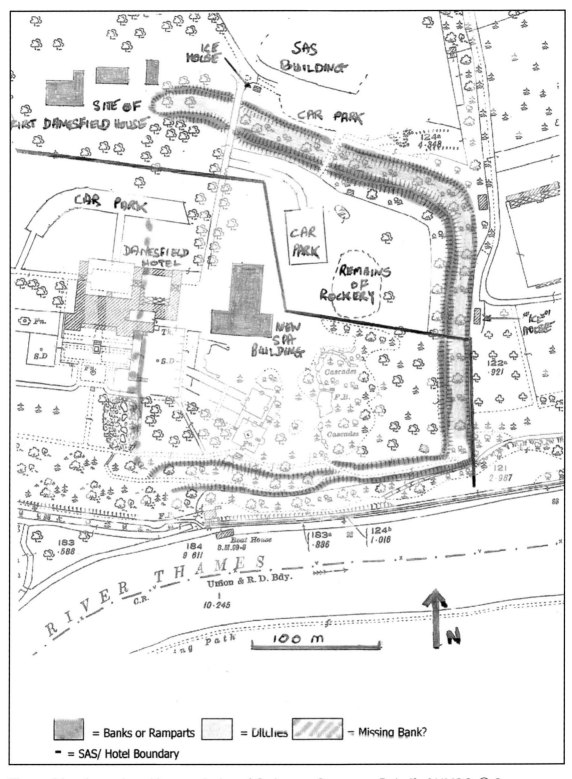

**Figure 31** *(reproduced by permission of Ordnance Survey on Behalf of HMSO. © Crown copyright 2005. All rights reserved. Ordnance Survey License number 100044133)*

them. The inner bank is four to six metres and the outer bank two to three metres above the present ditch level. The east side of the inner bank continues with the ditch well below it (six to seven metres along the northern part of this bank). However, the dimensions of the bank and the ditch decline as they near the high escarpment overlooking the River Thames.

The southern part of the Hill Fort has a valley in the centre, much lower than where the eastern and western banks adjoin the top of the escarpment overlooking the Thames. The valley was evidently landscaped in Victorian times as 'The Cascades' and has recently been renovated for the benefit and pleasure of the Hotel's guests.

The western bank and ditch were mostly removed by the construction of the second Danesfield House and by the activities of the War Office/M.O.D. (see Figure 31, page 76).

In October and November 2007, ten and seven AIM members, respectively, assembled outside SAS UK's headquarters on crisp dry days (see photographs 32 and 33 on page 78). In October, AIM members fought through the undergrowth and climbed the inner bank near the north-east corner of the Hill Fort, about 100 metres from the footpath running through the bank. It had been decided to measure profiles of the banks and ditches by using an optical tool known as a Dumpy Level, which had been borrowed. In November another profile was measured about 50 metres from the footpath.

A few days after each visit, the readings that had been taken were plotted on to graph paper and two profiles were drawn on tracing paper. These drawings were scanned into a computer and enhanced to produce graphics (see figure 32, page 79).

On a snowy day in March 2008, a small group of AIM members visited the north-west part of the Hill Fort. This time a profile was measured using a Laser Level. A straight line was set up across the ditch and a 50 metre tape was run along this line (see photograph 34, page 80). The Laser Level was levelled (made exactly horizontal), pointed along the line, the 'laser dot' was located on the graduated staff and a reading was noted every metre onto a pre-designed form. These readings were then converted into figure 33 page 80. These measurements show a differential of 3.5 metres from top to bottom, which is a fairly impressive figure even after more than 2,000 years of wear and tear!

In mid-April 2008, six AIM members visited the same area as in March (see photograph 35, page 81). The Total Station was erected and positioned on the southern bank and its position recorded. Then three ranging poles were inserted in the southern bank in a straight line and the Optical Square (for measuring exact right-angles) was used to position another pole on the bank of the other side of the ditch. Subsequently, four of AIM's 50 metre tapes were used to lay out 22 metre strips. These tapes were laid out two metres apart and measurements taken at two metre intervals along each tape; these were then recorded into the machine's memory. Once all the readings had been taken along the 50 metre tapes, three of them were wound up and then relaid to the east of the remaining tape, again two metres apart. Due to the presence of a large holly bush, only 16 metre strips could be recorded, again at two metre intervals (see figures 35, 36 and 37, pages 82 and 83).

## Danesfield Iron Age Hill Fort - Happy volunteers involved in 'profile surveying' using the Dumpy Level

**Photographs 32 and 33**

## Danesfield Iron Age Hill Fort - Bank and ditch profiles recorded in north-east sector

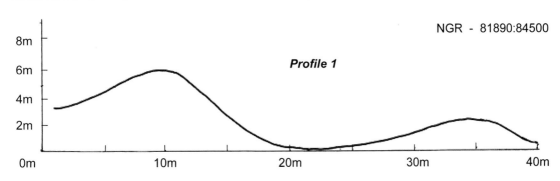

NGR - 81890:84500

Profile 1

8m
6m
4m
2m

0m          10m          20m          30m          40m

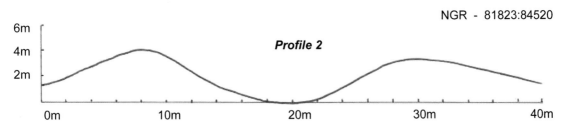

NGR - 81823:84520

Profile 2

6m
4m
2m

0m          10m          20m          30m          40m

**Figure 32**

## Danesfield Iron Age Hill Fort - Using the Laser Level in March 2008

to produce
the
'Profile',
below

Photograph 34

## Danesfield Iron Age Hill Fort - Profile, measured using a Laser Level, of north-west bank and ditch. GPS reading taken at 0 metres = NGR 81676:84543

**Danesfield Profile 23/3/08**

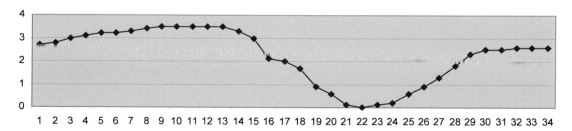

Figure 33

80

## Danesfield Iron Age Hill Fort - Surveying using the Total Station

Photograph 35

## In April 2008, at the North-west part of Danesfield Iron Age Hill Fort (NGR 8167:8454), the Total Station was used to produce three maps

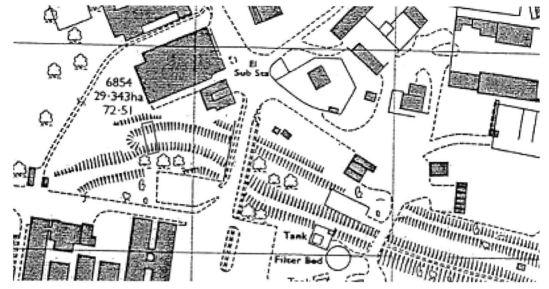

**Figure 34**  *(reproduced by permission of Ordnance Survey on Behalf of HMSO. © Crown copyright 2005. All rights reserved. Ordnance Survey License number 100044133)*

The red rectangle on the map above shows the area surveyed. The Contour Map below, shows every position at which a reading was recorded. Even today, over 2000 years since the Hill Fort's construction, there is a four metre differential between the top (white) and the bottom of the bank (orange).

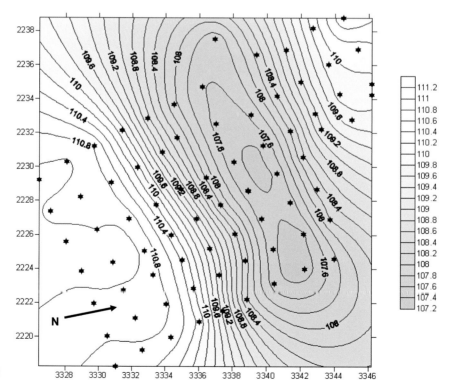

**Figure 35**

The Wire Frame map below, shows the southerly bank (blue), the ditch and the opposite bank. The top left and bottom right corners of the map are additions calculated by the computer programme in order to complete the graphic.

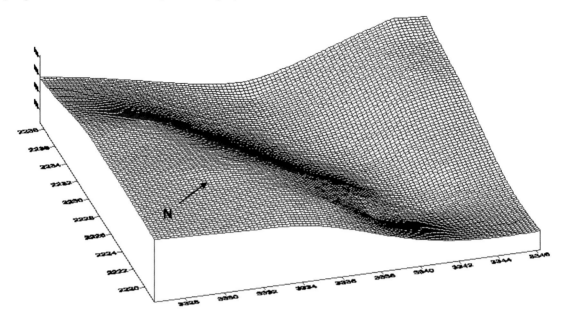

**Figure 36**

The Surface Map below, shows the southerly bank (blue), the bottom of the ditch (light green) and the top of opposite bank (light blue). The top left and bottom right corners of the map are additions, again calculated by the computer programme in order to complete the graphic.

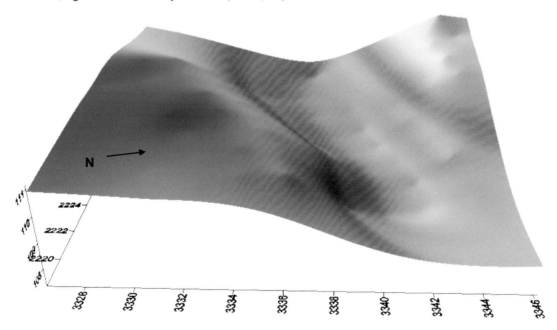

**Figure 37**

## Serendipity

Other methods of surveying were investigated, including LIDAR (LIght Distance And Ranging) as a possible way of mapping an overgrown terrain. This technique uses aircraft to map out sites that have heavy shrub and tree growth. AIM discovered that a company called Blue Skies had already produced LIDAR maps of the Danesfield area. Therefore, a small amount of the grant was invested on the purchase of the results of their endeavours.

Figures 38, below, and 39 on page 85, show a Lidar 'vegetation map' and a Lidar '3D map'.

### Danesfield Iron Age Hill Fort - Lidar '3D including vegetation' view

"LIDAR data Copyright Environment Agency Geomatics 2008"

**Figure 38**

## Danesfield Iron Age Hill Fort - Lidar '3D' view

"LIDAR data Copyright Environment Agency Geomatics 2008"

**Figure 39**

## Conclusions

Today 70% of the Danesfield Hill Fort is still in existence and the eastern and northern bank and ditch complexes are still impressive.

Previous investigations have dated this Hill Fort to the mid-Iron Age (approximately 2,350BC). Its relationship with the neighbouring Hill Fort at Medmenham is unsure, as the latter is, so far, undated.

Being so close to the River Thames, it is possible that this Hill Fort acted as a toll gate to gather taxes from those using the Thames as a highway. Alternatively, it could have acted as a trading post, especially as the mid-part of the river side of the Hill Fort is much lower than the other three sides, giving relatively easy access.

This Hill Fort is testament to the fortitude, expertise and determination of our ancestors. A large workforce of up to 200 people, working away for many years, would have been needed to construct this massive structure, using only rudimentary tools, such as 'antler picks'.

# Bibliography

Albion Archaeology, 2006. *Danesfield Conservation Management Plan.*

Archaeology In Marlow, 2003 to 2005. *Investigation Reports for SAS.*

Cocks A H, 1911. *The Danes' Ditches at Danesfield (Medmenham).* Records of Bucks Vol 10.

Michael Farley Archaeology, 1982. *Excavation Report for Danesfield House Hotel & Spa.*

Langley, Thomas, 1797. *The History and Antiquities of the Hundred of Desborough and Deanery of Wycombe in Buckinghamshire.* London.

Lipscomb, George, 1847. *The History and Antiquities of the County of Buckingham.* London: John & William Robins.

Northampton Archaeology, 1998. *Investigation Report for SAS.*

Oxford Archaeology, 1990 and 1997. *Excavation Reports for Danesfield House Hotel and Spa.*

Plaisted, Arthur H, 1925. *The Manor and Parish Records of Medmenham, Bucks. Medmenham*: The Village Bookshop,

Plaisted, Arthur H, 1958. *The Romance of a Chiltern Village – 5,000 BC to 1957 AD. Medmenham*: The Village Bookshop,

Royal Commission on Historic Monuments (England), 1912. *Buckinghamshire Vol. 1.* HMSO.

Sites and Monuments Record, 1996. *"Danesfield Camp No. 27156."* English Heritage.

**Thanks and acknowledgements to**

Archaeology in Marlow is extremely grateful that the Local Heritage Initiative (LHI) awarded the ROMADAM (Recording Of Marlow And District's Ancient Monuments) Project, a grant of £22,605 to survey four earthwork sites close to Marlow. The money granted by LHI allowed these investigations to proceed.

English Heritage for their help and permissions
The Local Heritage Initiative for Funding the ROMADAM Project
SAS UK for allowing us to have access to their land
Danesfield Hotel and Spa Centre for allowing us to have access to their land
Sandy Kidd (Senior Archaeologist for Buckinghamshire) for his advice and help
Albion Archaeology
Blue Sky Services
Mr Trevor Bownass for lending AIM his Dumpy Level and staff
David Greenwood for his research work on Danesfield Hill Fort
AIM members, Dave Greenwood, Gerry Platten, Dave Axworthy, Ray Balkwell, Ann Pitwell, Eileen Bottjer, Brian Vallis, Julie Rushton, Robert Dunsmuir, Peter Ricketts, Andrew Wallace & Mike Hyde
The many other members of AIM and members of the public who helped on the Project, especially those who helped to proof-read this book.

------------